ONE LIFE TO LIVE

Legacy

To David + Sabine

Live Your Legacy

Gal. 2:20

ONE LIFE TO LIVE

Legacy

DR. FRANK COX
FOREWORD BY LARRY WYNN

Printed in Canada

ISBN: 1-888-237-66-X

Cover design by Design Type, Lawrenceville, Georgia

DEDICATION

This book is dedicated to the very people who have invested in and influenced my life. Because of them, my life has been enjoyable and enriched.

To my wife, Mary, who is God's greatest gift to me. You are my laughter when I am low and my joy in life. You are the best when it comes to ministering by my side. Your sweet love for God and people will always be your legacy. Through the demands of ministry you have been a steady strength to help me become the man of God He created me to be. I love you with all my heart.

To Stephen and Brooke for being a young couple whose home and hearts are dedicated to the Lord. Your love for Jesus is admirable and your obedience is contagious. Always be humble as God uses you. There will be no surprise in this dad's life as you build a life of legacy.

To Jonathan who is a great inspiration to his dad. I am your biggest cheerleader and prayer warrior. I have watched you handle some great disappointments with dignity and godly character. I have admired your willingness to stand alone when needed and to do what is right. Jon, you will succeed in life because you discover the best in all and your greatest joy is seeing others win. This kind of life always builds a strong legacy. You are building a life that counts. You are going to make a great impact.

To Kristen who by far is one of the shining examples of godliness. Your heart is bent toward your heavenly Father. Only God could be more proud than your earthly dad. Your desire for holiness will create a legacy that matters. Oh, how God is going to use you!

TABLE OF CONTENTS

Acknowledgements 9

Foreword by Rev. Larry Wynn 13

1. A Call to An Extraordinary Life 15

2. Mama Loved Race Cars 19

Biblical Legacies

3. Noah: The Favored One 33

4. Abraham: The Friend of God 51

5. David: A Man after God's Heart 69

6. Enoch: Walked with God 95

7. Shadrach, Meshach, and Abednego:
   The Semper Fidelis Gang 115

Modern Day Legacies

8. Blessed Brokenness 137

9. When False Gods Give No Answers 149

10. Dying to Live 169

Endnotes 187

About the Author 191

To order additional copies
or to view other material by Dr. Frank Cox
www.northmetro.net

ACKNOWLEDGEMENTS

Without the help and assistance of many people, this book would not have become a reality. In the space provided, I want to express my gratitude for their investment in my life.

A professor at New Orleans Baptist Theological Seminary once stated, "Everything and everyone we meet in life will become a part of us!" I have found this to be a true statement. I have met some tremendous people over the years that have made an indelible impression on me, and that have left my life richer because of their influence.

First, my mom and dad, DeWitt and Edna Cox who have instilled their values into their son and even continue to do so to this day. They are the real deal. I have been fortunate in regards to whom God chose to be my parents. They have always sought to follow God and have desired to pass on their love for our heavenly Father. They have run the race with dedication and dependability second to none. I am so proud they are determined to reach their goal to finish well for Christ.

There have been many preachers who have taken time to be my friend and mentor. Some have walked through some deep valleys with me as encouragers. At moments of celebration they have been there to cheer me on. Their names to me read like giants in the faith. I appreciate their friendships more than they will ever know. They are Larry Wynn, Ike Reighard, Junior Hill, Bill Stafford, J. Robert White, Danny Watters, Wayne Hamrick, Joe H. Cothen, Landrum Leavell, Jerry Vines, Fred Wolfe, Sam Cathey, Jerry Falwell, David Ring, Rick Stanley and many others. Their imprint on my ministry and walk will be forever found.

I am an old athlete at heart. There have been friends who are coaches who have impressed me with their friendship and wise counsel when needed. Thames Coleman was my coach in high school. He sought to instill character in the boys who played for him. He taught us many life lessons that even to this day guide my life. The friendship of other coaches over the years has added great value as I have watched them deal with adversity. A friend like Ray Goff, former head coach of the University of Georgia, has been a tremendous encourager. Alan Fahring, former head coach at Collins Hill High School in Gwinnett County, Georgia is one of my best friends. He has taught me a great deal about leadership and being a true and trusted friend. Larry Sherrill, current head coach at Collins Hill High School, has allowed me (as did Coach Fahring) the privilege of being Chaplain for the football team. He is a quiet, gentle and determined man who is concerned about the character development of the boys who run out each Friday night to face victory and/or adversity. He is a great trainer of young men. To me there is nothing purer than high school football.

I have worked with some of the finest people in the ministry. Over the years I have enjoyed the fellowship of some godly men who have helped me grow one of the greatest churches in America. They have aided me in becoming who I am as pastor, preacher and leader. Thanks to Ken Sorrell, Alvin Hobgood, John Drake, Thad Smith, Tim Dowdy, Gale Coleman, Steve Andrews, Keith McBroom, Richard Brown, Chris Blanton, Juan Sali, Tom Gilliam, Steve Bullard, James Chastain, Glenn Canup, Mike Ashburn and Stephen Cox. They have been some of the best.

I want to thank Coach Billy Wells, an Honors English

teacher and football coach at Collins Hill High School, for his assistance in editing. His friendship has meant a great deal over the years and I appreciate his willingness to help in this project.

Thanks to my secretary, Buddi Gammage, for the transcribing and typing of dictations concerning this project and for her daily assistance in the Pastor's office at North Metro.

This project could not have been without the skills of Cheryl Mahr. She has dedicated herself to learning more than she wanted to know about typesetting, layouts and publishing. Thanks, Cheryl, for all that you did to make this book a reality.

Life is made up of stories, quips and quotes. There is one that speaks volumes to me. We're all familiar with the proverbial turtle sitting on top of a fence post. Believe me, the turtle had help getting there. Well, I have benefited from the assistance of many. I am honored they have invested in me.

FOREWORD By Rev. Larry Wynn

Everyone is building a legacy. What you leave behind in the way of this legacy is far more important than what you acquire in this life. Dr. Frank Cox in *Legacy, One Life to Live*, does an extraordinary job explaining the value of a life committed to God's plan and purpose. One very important conclusion comes through very clearly on each page of this book. The person who seeks God's approval above all else leaves a legacy friends and family alike can follow. *Legacy* connects with you through powerful lessons learned from great people of the faith like Noah, Abraham, David and others. Frank does a masterful job painting a picture of these heroes of the faith. He describes their successes and their failures in a way that is true to Scripture and personal to the reader who desires to live his life wisely while here on earth.

Frank also shares with the reader personal stories from the lives of contemporary people of faith who have determined to make life count for something that will last. The reader is given a glimpse into some of the storms and challenges those individuals have faced and how God has used these experiences to mold and shape the men and women, whose stories are told, into legacy builders.

Last but certainly not least, the heart of the writer comes through in every chapter. Frank Cox, as a pastor, mentor, husband, friend, and father, is committed to living his life for Jesus Christ in such a way that inspires others. This commitment is seen throughout the book. Frank's personal insight into the Scripture combined with his humor and scholarly, yet down to earth style makes *Legacy* appealing to all who read it. This is a must read for anyone whose desire it is to live life in a manner that counts for today and all eternity.

Rev. Larry Wynn
Senior Pastor
Hebron Baptist Church
Dacula, Georgia

A CALL TO AN EXTRAORDINARY LIFE

The real tragedy of life is not being limited to one talent,
but in the failure to use the one talent.

Anonymous

*J*onathan Edwards was an ordinary man that God used in an extraordinary way. He was totally surrendered to the Lordship of Jesus Christ. When he was young he chose not to waste his life. Instead, he allowed God to mold and use him for maximum impact.

Edwards was greatly used from the early stages of his life. At age ten, he wrote an essay on the nature of the soul. At thirteen, he entered what is now Yale University and in 1720 graduated valedictorian of his class. God had blessed him with gifts and abilities and Edwards made the most of God's blessings.

He was a powerful pulpiteer during his day. For those who heard him preach, it became obvious that God had placed His anointing upon Edwards' life. He preached his sermon, *Sinners in the Hands of an Angry God,* and a revival movement began to spread throughout New England. Congregations who heard this message would rise up from their seats weeping and moaning as conviction fell upon their hearts. This particular movement became known as The Great Awakening and impacted much of New England for sixty to seventy years. The key to his life was simple. Jonathan

Edwards had made a resolve as a young man. Describing his resolve Edwards wrote, "Resolved, that I will do whatsoever I think to be most to God's glory, in my own good, profit and pleasure, and the whole of my duration, without any consideration of the time, whether now, or never so many myriad of ages hence. Resolved, to do whatever I think to be my duty and most for the good and advantage of mankind in general. Resolved, to do this, whatever difficulties I meet with, how many so ever, and how great so ever."[1] He had a resolve to follow God with all his heart. Whether others did or not, he would.

Many do not know that a common characteristic among those who God uses is a passionate resolve. It seems as though they know that if they are going to make a difference, they must totally sell out to Jesus. They redeem time and use it to bring honor and glory to God. Jonathan Edwards' legacy was to live for God and make the most of the time God would give him here on the earth.

GOD GIVES EACH OF US DEFINING MOMENTS THAT DEMAND WE TAKE ACTION THAT NOT ONLY SHAPES OUR DESTINY BUT IMPACTS OUR WORLD FOR GOD.

Every one of us has a "God-appointed time" here on earth. We must wisely use the time for God. We must redeem the time as instructed in God's precious Word, making the most of it.

The ancient Greeks had a unique understanding of time. They spoke of time as more than just *chronos* from which we get the word chronological. They spoke of time in a different way, *kairos*. When they would use that term they were referring to time as moments filled with opportunity. Author James Emery White writes, "Kairos is time filled with opportunity, a moment pregnant with eternal significance and possibility."[2] Think about it for a moment. God gives each of us defining moments that demand we take action that not only shapes our destiny but impacts our world for God. When our chronological time is done, we should have built a God-honoring legacy.

Every true follower of Christ must understand we only have one life to live; therefore, we must seize the time appointed to us and use it for Him. We must seize the day!

In the critically acclaimed movie, *Dead Poets Society*, there are some powerful scenes that give attention to peoples' legacies in life. The English teacher, John Keating (played by Robin Williams) leads his students into the field of literature. One student is asked to read a line from a poem famed by Robert Herrick,

Gather ye rosebuds while ye may,
old time is still a-flying
and this same flower that smiles today,
tomorrow will be dying.[3]

Immediately Keating interjects the idea of *Carpe Diem*. He asks his students, "Who knows what it means?" A student in the front of the class says, "It means to seize the day."

The teacher in this scene probed the students even more as to why the writer would leave such an image in the reader's mind. After a wrong answer, the teacher gives this answer, "Because we are food for worms, lads, because believe it or not, each and every one of us in this room is one day going to stop breathing, turn cold and die."[4]

In another moving scene he has the class to look into a case full of photographs. He reminds them of those who have preceded them at the school and how they seized their opportunities. As the boys were captivated by these pictures, Keating said, "...if you listen real close, you can hear them whisper their legacy to you. Go on, lean in, and listen. You can hear it."[5] Then the teacher whispers, "Carpe...Carpe...Carpe Diem! Seize the day, boys, make your lives extraordinary."

> **GOD DESIRES EACH OF US TO LIVE EXTRAORDINARY LIVES**

God desires each of us to live extraordinary lives. He wants to use each and every one of us. For us to have maximum impact in our world, we must join Jonathan Edwards with the resolve to follow God with all our heart, whether others do or not. Remember you only have one life to live. What will be your legacy when everything is said and done?

MAMA LOVED RACE CARS

Yet you do not know what your life will be tomorrow.
You are just a vapor that appears for a little while
and then vanishes away.
James

*I*n the movie *Gladiator* there is a poignant scene in which the transfer of power is about to take place. The Roman Empire has just won a major victory over Germania, and the reigning Caesar knew death was imminent. His son and daughter had traveled to the battle front to be with their dad. Their motives at best were questionable. The son knew in the fantasy of his mind he was about to be named Caesar. Flashes of grandeur filled his thoughts. He was so close, but little did he know how far away he really was from his life's dream of being the Emperor.

The reigning Caesar, facing death, searched his soul and knew he could not appoint his son. He was faced with a monumental decision which only he could make. Who would be the next Caesar?

In his royal army was a general named Maximus. He was a leader of men, a man's man. The Emperor had seen not only his military bravery, brilliance and courage, but also his character and integrity. In the depths of his heart, the Emperor knew there was only one who was fit to be the next Caesar; it was Maximus.

The scene was moving as he offered to Maximus the emperorship of the Roman Empire. The general had only one desire, and it was not to lead the vast empire but to return to his home and family. In a stirring appeal, the Emperor looked

> **WHEN A MAN SEES HIS END, HE WANTS TO KNOW THERE WAS A PURPOSE TO HIS LIFE.**

into the eyes of Maximus and said, "I am dying, Maximus. When a man sees his end, he wants to know there was a purpose to his life."[1] The Emperor wanted to know his life counted. In that one statement, the legacy of a life is raised. Every one of us will leave a legacy behind that will mark our life in history. The question that every person must live with is the one raised by the Emperor – "Has my life had purpose?" Then the Emperor closed the scene with a question, "How will the world speak my name in years to come?"[2]

What a powerful question! In the book, *What Should I Do With My Life?* author Po Bronson makes a strategic observation. He says, "We are all writing the story of our life. We want to know what it's about, what are its themes, and which theme is on the rise. We demand of it something deeper or richer or more substantive. We want to know where we are headed, not to spoil our own ending by ruining the surprise, but we want to ensure that when the ending comes, it won't be shallow. We will have done something. We will not have squandered our time here."[3] Every person I've ever met in my life had one common thread; everyone wants to make a difference with their life.

Over the years I have spent some time in cemeteries because of my role as a minister. I've noticed the surroundings, no matter the cemetery, are always the same. There are head markers which carry a name of the person buried there. Behind each name is a story. Some are good while others are bad. Some are exciting and I guarantee you there are some that are pretty boring. However, each story is significant because it marks the existence of a person and their influence in a defined time.

If time permits, I love walking through cemeteries and reading the different head markers. When you read the head marker certain information is listed. A name will appear along with the date of birth followed by the date of death. There is something else which always appears on the head marker and is hardly ever noticed by the casual eye. It is called a hyphen. It is just a short line between the date of birth and the date of death. To me, it is the most important item on the marker. It represents the legacy, the very influence of a real person who lived a real life over real time. Think about it. It marks their whole life, their entire story on earth. Oh, the memories!

On July 4, 1986 my wife, Debbie, died of a malignant brain tumor at twenty-seven years of age. The head marker reads...Debra A. Cox, December 12, 1958 - July 4, 1986. There are times I will go and visit her grave. As I stand there, I just stare at the name and the dates. As I look at the hyphen, it represents a lot of memories, a life well lived, one which brought much glory to God.

William Shakespeare writes in the *Seven Ages of Man*, that "All the world's a stage, and all the men and women merely players; they have their exits and their entrances."[4] After you exit this world and your family and friends visit your grave and stare at your hyphen, what legacy will they review in their minds? The way you live life will determine whether it was a significant life which fulfilled its purpose. Will you have lived a life of impact, or will you have ended up shallow as Po Bronson wrote, a person who squandered their time here on earth, a total waste. You have no control over any of the information which will be listed on the marker except one. Ponder it for a moment. You had no input into your name. You did not control the date you came into this world and will not control the date you will exit. The only control you have is the hyphen, how you're going to live your life.

With each passing day you are building your legacy. Don't waste the brief time in history your Creator has given you upon this earth. James, the Lord's half brother, tells us about the brevity of life...

> *Come now, you say, 'Today or tomorrow we will go to such and such a city, and spend a year there, and engage in business and make a profit.' Yet, you do not know what your life will be like tomorrow. You are just a vapor that appears for a little while and then vanishes away. (James 4:13-14)*

I want you to let that verse settle into your heart and into the depths of your spirit. Maybe a different translation will help.

> *How do you know what will happen tomorrow, for your life is like the morning fog. It's here a little while, then it is gone. (James 4:14 NLT)*

Our time is short like the morning dew as it refreshes the earth, which is only here until the sun's heat evaporates the moisture and the dew disappears. The greatest gift God has given you is life and what you make of it is your greatest gift to God.

Mama Loved Race Cars

I am a bottom-line preacher. You can live a wasted life or a wise life. It's your choice. May I suggest to you only a life committed to Jesus in love, devotion, and service will bring glory to God and leave a legacy that will keep making a difference after you are long gone.

A TURNING POINT

> ... WE LIVE LIFE FORWARD BUT ONLY AS WE LOOK BACKWARDS DO WE UNDERSTAND LIFE.

It has been said that we live life forward but only as we look backwards do we understand life. Every person can look back over their life and realize decisions and choices were made that determined their life's path. They will also testify that what led them to certain decisions were important events that took place that shaped them as a person. These events are called turning points.

Several years ago I had one of those interesting experiences that proved to be a turning point. It propelled me to consider what the Scripture teaches about leaving a legacy after your life is completed here on earth. The experience presented itself to me through a dear lady's funeral. My phone rang with an urgent call from Bill Head, a funeral director in our county. He said, "Frank, we have a 52-year-old lady who has passed away. She is Baptist, new to the area, and does not have a church home. The family has heard about you and would like for you to conduct the service." I said, "Bill, she is Baptist, right?" Odd question, like that would make any difference. He assured me she was and I agreed to conduct her memorial service. The funeral would be at 11:00 the next morning. I rehearsed the Baptist funeral on my way to the funeral home. You probably know it well. Mama loved Jesus. Mama gave her life to Christ. The Scripture says, *absent from the body is to be present with the Lord*. It is a simple message but one that brings comfort for those who know the Lord. I was about to learn never to assume anything about a person's legacy. I was about to experience a turning point.

I arrived at the funeral home my customary ten minutes before the hour. I was greeted at the front door by the funeral director who took me and introduced me to the husband of the deceased and their two grown children. After a few condolences, I asked if we could go to the conference room for a minute so I could ask a few questions in order to make the memorial service as personal as I could.

As we entered the room, I took a seat at the head of the conference table with the husband at the opposite end. The two children sat on each side. "Sir" I said, "I want to make this as personal as possible. I noticed your wife was Baptist. Please tell me when she received Christ as her personal Savior." To be honest, I was not prepared for what I was about to hear. He said, "Received Christ? Preacher, we are pagans. We don't believe in that Jesus garbage and whatever you do, please don't bring Jesus up in this funeral today." Immediately my nice little funeral message flew right out the window. What was I to do? My father, also a Baptist preacher, always taught me when you are in doubt, put the question back to them. "Well, sir, what do you want me to say for your friends who have gathered to remember your wife?" The husband thought for a moment, looked at his children and then responded, "Tell them she loved race cars." At first I didn't believe I heard what he said correctly. In fact, I heard myself saying, "Do what?" "Tell them she loved race cars?" I wrote it down, stood up and said, "Sir, you may not believe in Jesus but I do. You may not need Christ today, but I do and I would like to lead us in prayer." He said, "Do whatever you want to do." So I prayed a short prayer for God's guidance and for the Lord to give me the right words to say during this sweet lady's funeral.

Returning to the viewing room, we had prayer again with the family members before going to the chapel. As we walked down the aisle of the chapel, I kept running through my mind the phrase, "Mama loved race cars." I took my seat on the platform and the soloist began singing *Beulah Land*. I thought, "Buddy, if you only knew you wouldn't be singing *Beulah Land*." I kept flipping through my Bible to see what God's Word said about race cars. Do you know it says nothing about race cars?

As the soloist wound down on *Beulah Land*, I rose to my feet and took the three or four steps to the podium. I used for my text the rich man in hell:

> *Now there was a rich man and he habitually dressed in purple and fine linen, joyously living in splendor every day. And a poor man named Lazarus was laid at his gate covered with sores and longing to be fed with the crumbs which were falling from the rich man's table. Besides even the dogs were coming and licking his sores. Now the poor man died and was carried away by the angels to Abraham's bosom, and the rich man also died and was buried. In Hades he lifted up his eyes, being in torment, and saw Abraham far away, and Lazarus in his bosom, and he cried out and said, 'Father Abraham, have mercy on me and send Lazarus so that he may dip the tip of his finger in water and cool off my tongue, for I am in agony in this flame!' And Abraham said, 'Child,*

25

*remember that during your life you received good
things, and likewise, Lazarus, bad things, but now
he is being comforted here and you are in agony. And
besides all this, between us and you there is a great
chasm fixed, so that those who wish to come over
from here to you will not be able, and that none may
cross over from there to us. And he said, 'Then I beg
you, father, that you send him to my father's house,
for I have five brothers in order that he may warn
them, so that they will not also come to this place of
torment.' But Abraham said, 'They have Moses and
the Prophets; let them hear them.' But he said, 'No,
father Abraham, but if someone goes to them from
the dead, they will repent.' But he said to him, 'If
they do not listen to Moses and the Prophets, they
will not be persuaded even if someone rises from the
dead.' (Luke 16:19-31)*

With the Scripture read I took a deep breath and heard
myself ask, "If this dear lady could speak from where she is
today, what would she say?" Now before you condemn me
for having no compassion, realize that nine people came to
know Christ as their personal Savior at this lady's funeral.

After the message and prayer, the family wanted to
open the casket and allow the people to file by one last time. I
took my place at the head of the casket as people (friends and
family) came and paid their respects then moved on to the
parking lot to travel the few miles to the cemetery. The funeral
director came to close the casket, and I told him, "Bill, wait a
minute, we're missing someone." He said, "With a crowd like
this you can tell someone didn't come by?" I said, "Yes, the

husband." Around the flowers he came. I'm not the smartest preacher in the world, but I noticed something was different about the husband. He had gone and changed suits. During the funeral he was wearing a blue suit and now he was wearing a tan suit. As he walked toward me and the casket, he was rolling the blue suit into a tight bundle. He took a quick look at his deceased wife and then proceeded to stuff the suit into the casket. He looked at me and said, "She hated that suit." I said, "What?" "She hated that suit. She hated these shoes. If I knew I could get by with going to the cemetery without shoes, I would stick these shoes along with the suit into this casket and let her carry them to wherever she is today."

As I said, this was a turning point. This dear lady's funeral service changed my life. I walked away thinking how sad to live 52 years and all that could be said is that you loved race cars. The only thing of value about her life was she loved a pile of metal containing an engine. I believe this would be described as a shallow life, maybe even one that had been squandered.

... MOST ARE LIVING LIFE TODAY WITH NO THOUGHT OF THE LEGACY THEY WILL LEAVE BEHIND.

However, the truth is most are living today with no thought of the legacy they will leave behind. They are aiming at nothing and are hitting it every time. They leave memories of a life which seemingly had no purpose. Remember James says you're here today and gone tomorrow.

I returned to my office after the funeral disturbed by what I had just witnessed. As I thought through my experience I turned to the Word of God. Then it dawned on me. God is big into legacies. It is important to our Creator how we live our lives. He watches everything we do, listens to everything we say, and records for eternity the legacy of our lives. You ask, "How do you know this?" Well, the Scripture bears this out for us. It says...*Noah found favor in the sight of God.* From the very heart of God, He describes Noah's legacy. Abraham was a friend of God, a legacy. David was a man after God's own heart. Legacy! The one I like is Enoch. He walked with God. Yes, God is big into legacies.

The question one must consider is what will others say about you when your life is over? Better yet, what will God say about you? By now I hope you are asking the question, what is the point? It is rather simple. What you do with your life is really important. Each of you will leave a legacy behind. In fact, your legacy will even precede you into eternity. That is a sobering thought.

WHAT WE DO IN THIS LIFE WILL ECHO THROUGHOUT ETERNITY!

The night I watched the movie *Gladiator* with my family, I was enthralled with one particular scene before a great battle. Maximus was in full control of his men. The time for battle was at hand. He knew the words he spoke could inspire his men to victory. As he mounted his horse and made a couple of quick turns to view his men he shouted these words, "What we do in this life will echo throughout eternity!"[5] It is important for us to realize that our lives have meaning to God. Our existence here is not insignificant to Him.

Quickly travel with me back to that scene where the Caesar was turning over his kingdom to Maximus. In that powerful moment the emperor looked into the eyes of Maximus and said, "I am dying, Maximus. When a man sees his end he wants to know there was a purpose to his life."[6]

Mama Loved Race Cars

Then the emperor asked a penetrating question I pose to you as you read this book. He asks, "How will the world speak of my name in years to come?"[7] I think each and every one of us must ponder that question. After you are long gone, what will your family and your fellow Christians say about you in the years to come?

Join me as we journey through the pages of the Bible and review some biblical legacies that have been given to us as examples. Read carefully the biblical legacies but also the chapters on modern-day legacy builders who are making a real difference for Christ through various circumstances of their lives. Allow these stories to inspire you to consider how you are living your life for Jesus Christ. It is my desire that when everything is said and done about your life, the minister who presides at your funeral can say more than just…you loved race cars.

Biblical Legacies

No life meaningfully linked to God can be utterly cast down.

Anonymous

3

NOAH: THE FAVORED ONE

*It is time for us Christians to face up
to our responsibility for holiness!*
Jerry Bridges

*B*iographical sermons are rich to preach. There is one I love to preach called *Legacy*. It's about building a life that makes a difference for God. Every believer must remember that God is big into the legacies we create with our lives. In the Scripture we're reminded that even God records our legacies for all eternity. It speaks of the great men of the faith like Noah, Abraham, David, and Enoch. It describes their legacies with sound bites…Noah found favor with God…Abraham was a friend of God…David was a man after God's own heart…and Enoch walked with God. This is the way God chose to record them for history. While our lives may not be found in the Bible, we are being marked forever.

As I studied some of these giants in the Bible my own life was enriched. I would see men I could relate to. They had struggles just like me and many times their lives were marked with failures, just like my own. I saw their characteristics and read what God said about each of them, and it strengthened my life. God uses a man like Noah to introduce me to the riches of His mercy. Saint Augustine said, "We count on God's mercy for our past mistakes, on God's love for our present needs, on God's sovereignty for our future." With God, every person has a future.

Here lies the genius of God. His Word introduces

us to men and women and upon close examination of their lives, you discover they are people just like us with feet of clay. They have great strengths and about the time you are rejoicing over their accomplishments, their weaknesses show up. He brings us alongside their lives and allows us to see their victories and defeats. To our amazement they prove to be an unholy bunch. I am sure we can all relate. One finds reassurance as you study these biblical people and discover something tremendous about God. If we will ever allow this truth to take root in our lives it will set us free. The truth I want you to realize is that God doesn't look at their holiness but God looks at His holiness that is within them. In other words, it's not about you, *it's not about what you can do for God. It's all about what God can do through you if you will just surrender your life to Him.* He constantly reminds me that He desires to use me, to my amazement. Through people like you and me He desires to mark our world with His righteousness.

THROUGH PEOPLE LIKE YOU AND ME, HE DESIRES TO MARK OUR WORLD WITH HIS RIGHTEOUSNESS.

The question becomes: what hinders us from being used by God? Many times we cannot be used by God because of our unbelief. We say, "Not me! God can't use me because I know my past and for sure God couldn't, no He wouldn't use me at all." Well, I have some good news for you. In every generation God looks upon the face of the earth and looks for people who are willing to stand against the tide of life. He is looking for those who are willing to stand tall for Him

GOD LOOKS UPON THE FACE OF THE EARTH AND LOOKS FOR PEOPLE WHO ARE WILLING TO STAND AGAINST THE TIDE OF LIFE.

when everybody in the world is going with the flow. If you're willing to do that, then you are the type of person that God desires and the very one He will use in a tremendous way.

Have you ever been to the ocean when there has been a strong undertow? You know what it's like when you're out there and you're trying to get back to land. You are swimming, or better yet, walking against the tide and you have this strange, if not panicky, feeling that the undertow is pulling you back out. At that point, you know it will demand every bit of energy to get back to shore, so you give it all you have in order to attain your goal. Well, God is looking for those who are willing to expend the necessary energy within their lives to make it safely to the other side of the shore of holiness by standing tall for the name of Jesus Christ.

In Hebrews 11, some great people of faith who, while not perfect, were willing to do what it would take to walk with God. In verse seven, God, through His writer, introduces us to Noah who was one of those special men. What God said about this man Noah is worthy of our attention. He says,

> *By faith Noah being warned by God about things not yet seen, in reference prepared an ark for the salvation of his household, by which he condemned the world and became an heir of the righteousness which is according to the faith. (Hebrews 11:7)*

The history of this verse is recorded in Genesis 6 in the Old Testament. There are two concepts that are important to know about the legacy of Noah, the one who found favor in the eyes of God.

THE DEFINING MARKS OF NOAH'S DAY

The first thing I want you to see is what I call the defining marks of Noah's day. If you understand these marks you will be able to understand the man. It will help us comprehend why the Bible says he found favor in the eyes of God.

Noah's time could be compared to our day. It was a day of *scandalous activity*. There is no soap opera that can do justice to the times of Noah. To know what was going on in Noah's day is enough to make one blush with embarrassment. For a pastor to stand in an open worship service and relate all the wickedness that was present would summon protest from the congregation. Some would rise to their feet and say, "Foul, Pastor! You shouldn't say those kinds of things within earshot of our children. We don't want our kids to hear that kind of talk!" When reading about Noah's day one discovers it reads like current events in the local newspaper. Our children are living in a real world that mirrors the days of Noah. We can call "foul" down at the church house, but what we need to do is get out there in our culture and cry "foul" for the way many are living their lives. Why is it that Christians cannot have such influence in our culture? Could it be that many of us are just like the people that surrounded Noah? We have compromised and winked at sin so long we have lost the ability to stand against the tide. In other words, we're in the rapids of the river and we're going with the flow instead of swimming upstream.

> **WE HAVE COMPROMISED AND WINKED AT SIN SO LONG WE HAVE LOST THE ABILITY TO STAND AGAINST THE TIDE.**

In Matthew 24 the gospel writer describes what it will be like when Jesus shall come again. When Christ ends the parable of the fig tree, He says it will be as in the days of Noah. Jesus says, "If you want to know when I'm about to come, all you will have to do is go back, look at the days of Noah and see what was taking place, and if your culture parallels that of Noah's day, then look up for Jesus is on His way!"[1]

A close look at Noah's day should cause us some concern. Do you know what kind of society it was? It was a pornographic society. Recently there was an interview on TV that caught my attention. They were asking a leading sociologist to describe our culture in one word. He said, "In a word I would say pornographic." We're living in a pornographic society. Jesus says it will be as in the days of Noah.

What marked Noah's time? There are three characteristics that marked his days. First, it was a day of *spiritual decline*. It can be said our society is in a spiritual decline. In America we are reminded that our nation believes in God. We look around and can see there are some great and tremendous churches sprinkled throughout our land that are full on Sunday mornings; however, it is one thing to go to church and quite another to live out your Christian life. It is one thing to show up for worship service because you have a deep desire to encounter God, and quite another to come because church is good entertainment. Many people look at our worship today as just a good show. Worship should be about bringing your life in concert with the righteousness of God and finding strength to walk faithfully with God in your every-day life. In Noah's time it was a day of spiritual decline. They may have ascribed to God and even talked about God, but they turned their backs on Him. If you walked up to them on the street and said, "Do you love God?" many would say,

"Oh yes, I love God." Faith has always been there in some form since Adam and Eve. It had been delivered to Adam. It was such a dynamic faith that the martyr Abel was prepared to shed his blood. That same kind of faith was disappearing in the days of Noah.

Is it not the same in our culture? Recently in a prayer meeting an older gentleman in our church and I were discussing the spiritual decline in America. I said, "Ray, I bet you never thought you would live to see our nation in the moral decline we're in today." He said, "I have seen things in the last five years that I never dreamed I would see and cannot even comprehend what the next five years will bring." The problem is spiritual decline. We can blame our society and believe me, this evil generation gives us enough ammunition to use. All we have to do is read the headlines of the daily paper or take a stroll through the internet. However, the real truth is convicting. The problem lies within those who claim Jesus as Lord. We are the ones who are commanded to be salt and light. We are to flavor and influence our culture. Yet, there are those in the Christian faith who say we believe one thing but do we practice what we really believe? Many times the two do not match at all.

We ought to be asking certain questions. Why are Christians not living in holiness and separation? Where are the saints who are trying to live for the Lord? What are we doing to make a difference for Jesus? These are questions which should cause every saint to realize how important it is to live out our profession of faith. The fact that one would have to ponder such questions should indicate we are in spiritual decline.

The other day I was reading a book on spiritual

Noah

awakening because I'm praying for spiritual awakening in my life and in the life of our church and in our culture. As I was studying the book written by Tom Phillips, I was impressed by a story he related. Tom was preaching at a spiritual awakening conference. As he was preaching, a lady was sitting on the front row listening to every word he had to say about spiritual awakening in America. He made the great declaration that he felt America was ripe for spiritual awakening and a fresh touch from God. When he did, she raised her hand. She said, "Mr. Phillips, I disagree. I don't think America is ready for a spiritual awakening." He said, "What do you mean?" She went on to say, "When I look around and see the collapse of families in our culture, the high divorce rate even among the church

> WE'RE A SOCIETY WHERE CHRISTIANS CANNOT WAIT TO GET HOME AFTER CHURCH ON SUNDAY, NOT TO PRAY OR STUDY GOD'S WORD, BUT TO WORSHIP THE DALLAS COWBOYS.

family and see young lives being ripped apart by drugs, sex, and drive-by shootings, a society with angry drivers and ugly graffiti and one major disaster after another, I don't believe we're ready for a spiritual awakening. When I recognize we're a society with starving people, bankrupt governments, and hurting friends, it is hard for me to fathom we're on the verge of spiritual awakening." Then she continued, "We're a society where Christians cannot wait to get home after church on Sunday, not to pray or study God's Word, but to worship the Dallas Cowboys." Why should that shock us? It is simple. We're living in the day of Noah which is characterized by spiritual decline.

The second characteristic is we are living in a day of

shameless depravity. We are living in a time when our society is taking everything that God has made beautiful and we have sought to pervert it. Take our view of marriage today. God has always intended for marriage to be between a man and a woman for life, but today we have changed marriage to fit our desires versus the plan of God. In Noah's day family values, as prescribed by God, were not high on their culture's list. Polygamy, same-sex marriages, or perversion were just as prevelant in that day as ours. The only difference is the legal twist our society applies to spiritual decline.

Let's stop and think about our culture for a moment. Some would say we are a monogamous society. You may ask, what does that mean? According to God's plan it is for one man to be married to one woman for life, until death do us part. We all promised something to that effect at our marriage ceremonies. As a society we would claim we practice monogamy; however, reality in America says we practice serial monogamy. We no longer believe in monogamy in the same way the Bible speaks. We're talking about monogamy in the way our society interprets it. Serial monogamy has been defined as one man and one woman married for a season, then they divorce and marry someone else. They are married for a season then divorce and marry someone else. That's the culture in which we live.

I understand there are times when divorce is a reality, where adultery has been committed and biblical grounds are met for divorce; however, it still doesn't take away the sting upon our culture and the lack of impact Christians have on the family front. Could it be that Christians in America have winked at heterosexual sin for so long that when it is time to stand against perversion, we do not have the moral background to stand up and stand against that which is tearing our culture apart?

In the day of Noah, it was a day of pornography and polygamy. It was also a day of perversion through homosexual sin. It was a day when people were giving over to their own lusts. Do you know in the American culture we're seeing the demise of the biblical view of marriage as God tells us in His Word? In the Book of Genesis chapters one and two, it speaks of how God created Adam and eventually Eve from the rib of man. God created Adam and Eve—nowhere does it say that God created Adam and Steve! In our country recent history tells us how far we are from God as a nation when the attempt was made to legalize same sex marriage. Christians by the millions slumber on in our complacency while unrighteousness crouches at the door and judgment arrives on the horizon. What you need to understand is that our culture is no different than Noah's.

J. Emmett Henderson, former specialist for Ethics and Public Affairs at the Georgia Baptist Convention, wrote an article to warn us concerning the perversion of same-sex marriages and its impact on our society. The headline reads, *Same-Sex Marriage Threatens Marriage Itself.* It speaks about how our society is collapsing in regards to the sanctity of marriage. Recently the Texas Supreme Court ruled Texas sodomy laws to be unconstitutional. This will have severe impact on sexual conduct, marriage, and the family for decades. It went on to tell us that according to Justice Scalia the state laws against same-sex marriage, bigamy, adult incest, prostitution, adultery, fornication, bestiality, and obscenity are all called into question by the decision of the Texas court. You, like me, cringe at something like that but do you know that in 1999 in Vermont, the Supreme Court of Vermont said that the state of Vermont had to observe or tolerate same-sex marriages? Do you know that at the same time of this writing, the Massachusetts Supreme Court has ruled to approve same-sex marriages? Do you know there is an agenda, a movement across our land, where the homosexual community is pushing with great intensity to have same-sex marriages approved in post-Christian America? It may be tolerated according to our perverted culture, but it goes against the Word of God. How appalling because of our perversion in America that on May 21, 2003, a resolution had to be brought before Congress supporting the biblical view of marriage! If it is not eventually passed, and if the homosexual agenda of our day is enacted into American law, we will witness the collapse of the family unit as we know it. I prophesy the total demise of American culture and this will invite the judgment of God as in Sodom and Gomorrah. As Christians we must be willing to stand against the tide of a culture that is perverted. We're living in the days of Noah. We're living in a day of shameless depravity.

Third, it is also a day of *strong delusion*. When you read through the life of Noah there is one thing that will grip your heart. It is found in the Book of Genesis and repeated in the life of Jesus Christ. In Matthew 24:39 it says that God was moving against the people and the people did not even recognize it. God is active and will bring judgment. Study the life of Noah in Genesis and you will discover how serious God was in bringing judgment upon Noah's contemporaries. The sad reality for Noah's day and ours is as God moved in Heaven, they did not know of it on earth. In Matthew 24:39 according to The Message translation, it says...

Noah

They knew nothing until the flood hit and swept everything away. (Matthew 24:39 The Message)

Man, what a society—one that had given itself over to sin and lustful desires. God was bringing judgment and yet their society knew nothing until the flood hit and swept everything away. Could it not be said of America in our day? It is a day of scandalous activity.

It was also a day of *sovereign accountability*. One needs to understand that God will not be fooled when it comes to accountability. There are three things I want you to take serious note of as we think of accountability.

> **GOD WILL NOT BE FOOLED WHEN IT COMES TO ACCOUNTABILITY.**

One, God took an *assessment*. He took an assessment here on the earth and the Scripture describes what He saw. It says…

And then the Lord saw the wickedness of man was great upon the earth…and the intent of man was only evil continuously. The impact was tremendous. The earth was filled with violence…and God looked on the earth and behold, it was corrupt. (Genesis 6:5-12)

As God took an assessment and measured it against His holiness, He was not pleased with the humanistic, materialistic, self-centered, and new age occultism of Noah's day. When one takes a passing look at our society today, it is easy to hear God. He could rightfully say, "I looked upon the earth and saw the wickedness of man was great on the earth…every intent of man's heart is evil continuously and the earth is filled with violence." Believe me, He sees corruption everywhere—the assessment of God.

However, it doesn't stop there. There is a second thing to notice, the *attitude* of God. The attitude of God could not be more displayed than found in Genesis 6:3. It says, "…then the Lord said 'My Spirit will not always strive with man.'" Could you imagine not having the power and the Spirit of God around your life? God says as He looks upon man and sees the shape the world is in, "My Spirit will not always strive with man." He was grieved to the heart that He had created man. He was broken over corrupt humanity and was committed to destroy them (Genesis 6:7). The point is that holy God will not allow rebellion, sin, and corruption to continue without bringing judgment and justice upon creation.

Now the argument goes, "…oh, that's in the days of Noah." But what does Jesus say? He says right before He returns it will be as in the days of Noah. God would not allow rebellion, sin, violence, and corruption to go without judgment and the same is true for our day. In the New Testament God says the Lord corrects those whom He loves. The Lord corrects those who call themselves children of God, those who are in the faith through Jesus Christ. If you are a child of God then you need to understand the attitude of God is that He will bring justice to your life (Hebrews 4:4-13). It is His moral integrity.

The third aspect of accountability to God is found in the *actions* of God. He does the assessment and the attitude of His heart is that He is grieved. God is broken that He made man and the action is His impending judgment. He is about to literally reign judgment from Heaven. A holy God cannot allow sin to go unchecked. He's going to bring judgment upon the sin of the world, yet we in America sleep on in our rebellion.

> **A HOLY GOD CANNOT ALLOW SIN TO GO UNCHECKED.**

THE DIVINE'S MENTION IN NOAH'S DAY

The defining marks of Noah's day leads one to consider what God says about Noah. Holy God brings up Noah's dedication. When I read about the judgment of God, here's the question I must ask: Is there not one who can be saved? God said take a look at Noah. Noah by faith prepared an ark condemning the world and that brought about the righteousness of God by faith. Notice two things concerning this man that God was willing to say.

First is what I call the *legacy* of Noah. When you study his life you see three things right up front.

A quick study and we become acquainted with the *testimony* concerning Noah. Genesis 6:8 says that after God said "I'm sorry that I made man" it reveals hope when it says "...but Noah found favor in the eyes of God." What a testimony! Wouldn't you like for it to be said that as God looks down upon this corrupt, wicked, evil generation that we find around us, He views your walk with Him and proclaims, "Ah, but there is one I see that I favor!" When God looked down and saw mass corruption, the Bible says He saw one man's correctness. As He gazed upon Noah, He bestowed His favor upon him. What does the word *favor* mean? A study of the Hebrew language of the Old Testimony paints a beautiful picture for us. In the midst of wickedness, evil, violence, and corruption, there was one who was swimming against the tide, standing when everybody else was bowing, that was aglow when everybody else had grown dull. God's eyes fell upon Noah and Noah received favor.

The word *favor* means grace and mercy. What greater legacy could be said about anyone than you received the grace and mercy of God? When everything is over in your life, they should know you were a person under the grace and mercy of God.

The legacy of Noah's family goes back to Genesis 4 where it tells us that Adam and Eve had another son named Seth and Seth had a son named Enosh. Then almost as a byline it simply states, "Men began to call upon the Lord" (Genesis 4:26). They began to seek God. At this point, I believe Noah sought the grace and mercy of God Almighty and God had bestowed His grace upon him. Noah found favor in the eyes of God!

It doesn't take long to discover the *traits* concerning Noah. Read carefully because it should be our desire that the same be said about each of us.

In Genesis 6:9ff there are certain traits mentioned concerning Noah. These traits are evident in people that find favor in the eyes of God. The Bible says these are the records of the generations of Noah. Listen to this first trait. Noah was a *righteous* man. What does that mean? It simply means that Noah was one that had right conduct and right integrity. He had integrity not only to his fellow man but he had integrity to the laws of God. When people look at your life, do they see that you are a person of integrity toward your fellow man? Do you have integrity toward the laws of God? Noah had upright character in a scandalous society. He had upright conduct in an unrighteous culture. When his culture was bending their knees to the world and to the whims of their day, it was Noah who was seeking God. It was Noah that had a mark of godliness upon his life. Just study his life and you will discover that he stands out from his contemporaries as a man of right behavior and one who enjoys a right relationship with God during a day of unrestrained evil. Even when he was preaching repentance to his generation, they laughed to his face, mocked and ridiculed this man of righteousness. When they left their angry mob and walked passed Noah, do you know what they probably thought about him? I promise many were thinking, "Now there is a man of God. He is a godly one." Should your desire not be the same? When people look at your life, yes, and even ridicule, mock, and scorn you as being out of touch because of your Christiaity, at least in the depths of their hearts they will know you to be a man or woman of God. Be willing to swim against the current!

The second trait was he was *blameless*. Do you know what the word *blameless* means? It means he was strong. It means he was a man who was sound. It was a word also used for those special animals they would bring to sacrifice to God in the Old Testament. They looked for those animals that were unblemished. Noah was that kind of man, without blemish. He was approved by God. Here is a question we need to ask: Did Noah sin? Sure he sinned. He is just like you and me. He was a man that had marks in his life that he was not proud of just like every man who has ever lived. I am sure there were activities in Noah's life that he would be totally embarrassed over. What did God mean when He said he was without blemish? It simply meant that he did not behave as the wicked of his day. He did not give his life over to the wickedness and the evil of his society and that trait distinguished him from his generation. He maintained fidelity and purity when all others were following the pack.

Now there is a third trait I want you to comprehend. He was a man who *walked* with God. This has only been said about two men in the Word of God. It was Enoch and Noah and the reason is simple.

Bruce Wilkerson, in his book *Set Apart*, gives a little insight in the beginning of the chapter entitled "I Want to be More Like Christ." Bruce Wilkerson quotes Jerry Bridges. Read slowly and ponder the words.

> *It is time for us Christians to face up to our responsibility for holiness. Too often we say we're defeated by this or that sin. No, we're not defeated, we're simply disobedient. It might be well if we stopped using the terms victory and defeat to describe our progress and holiness. Rather, we should use the terms obedience and disobedience.* [2]

When I read that quote, I looked at Noah's life and here's what I found. The reason God could say He found favor in Noah was because Noah quit trying to place blame for his sin elsewhere. No, he realized that the most important thing in anyone's life is their obedience to God and their walk with God.

The reason Noah was spared when everybody else outside the family was destroyed was because he was obedient to God. God came to him and told him, "Noah, get your tools and gather these supplies. I want you to build a boat for me because I'm going to bring flood waters and I'm going to

Noah

destroy the earth and everything under the heavens, every creature that has breath and life in it." The Bible says Noah obeyed God, then God said, "Noah, I want you to preach repentance and warn all the people." Noah was building the ark by day and he was preaching repentance at night and the people laughed, ridiculed, and mocked him. Do you know what the Bible says? The Scripture tells us he obeyed God. He would not turn against God. It did not matter when he heard the crowd crying out with criticism as he was working away on that ark. They would cry out, "Noah! Noah! What's the matter? Did you forget you live in a desert?" And then they would all laugh. Then somebody else would call out, "How are you going to get that monstrosity to the sea? Have you gone mad?" Yet every time Noah went back to the words he heard from God. With godly confidence, he remained obedient to his mission.

The traits of Noah should be our traits. He was righteous, blameless, and walked with God. Walking with God means to know Him and knowing God means to love Him, and to love God means to hear Him, and to hear God means to obey Him, and to obey God means salvation. Take that and apply it to Noah's life. Noah realized that the most important thing in his life was to make a strategic decision to walk with God. He knew it was not an event, but it was a process. Every day Noah walked with God. As he walked with God and listened, he knew God. As he came to know God more, he loved God more. As he loved God more, he heard God more. As he heard God more, he obeyed God. As he obeyed God, it brought salvation to his life.

Noah was favored by God. What a legacy! Will that be said about you?

Legacy

4

ABRAHAM:
THE FRIEND OF GOD

God carries a picture of you in His wallet.
Tony Campolo

*I*t is a stated fact that everyone is going to die. The mortality rate is one out of one. The only way to escape death is for the Rapture to occur. It would be wise to think about this occasion sooner rather than later. James, the writer of the book in the New Testament that bears his name, reminds us that life is like a vapor—here today and gone tomorrow (James 4:14). It is quick!

Junior Hill, an evangelist friend, says, "Life is like rewinding an audio cassette. It seems to start out real slow but the closer you get to the end, it seems to pass with lightning speed." How true his statement is when it is registered against the experience of life!

While we are on the subject, allow me to pose a question for your consideration. How will you be remembered? Better yet, how do you want to be remembered? What would be the one thing your minister would focus on as he speaks of the time between your birth and your death? I believe the greatest thing that could ever be said about anyone would be concerning their friendship and relationship with God. I would be honored if a minister could stand and say, "Frank was a friend of God." I have been told my whole life that I would be known by the company I keep. What a testimony if it could be said I kept company with God!

If there was ever a man in the Bible it could be said was a friend of the most high God, it would be Abraham. In the Scriptures you will discover an epitaph, a legacy concerning the life of Abraham. It was not a minister reminding us of this man's life, it was God speaking. God always speaks from His perfect knowledge. He says "Abraham was a friend of mine."

Have you ever thought about that word *friend*? Life is full of clichés. We have heard it said in order to have a friend you must be a friend. I believe we all try to be a friend to others. Do you know what a friend really is? Friendship can be summed up in three words. The words which quickly come to mind are those that measure every friendship. A friend is loyal, trustworthy, and committed. It is that simple. Those words describe what it takes to be a friend to people and it takes the same three words in action to be a real friend of God.

In Abraham's life you will find all three traits; however, there is another trait I would zero in on. He was totally sold out to God. How so? I would call Abraham God's "whatever friend." He was a friend that would say by his actions, "God, whatever you want me to do, wherever you want me to go, whatever you ask of me I will be obedient. I will be totally committed to your call upon my life." In Genesis 12 the testimony of this man is tremendous when it simply states, "...Abraham went forth as the Lord had commanded him." In Hebrews 11:8 the writer describes the obedience of Abraham regarding his friendship toward God when he says,

Abraham

By faith Abraham, when he was called, obeyed by going out to a place which he was to receive for inheritance and he went out not knowing where he was going.

By his willingness to trust God with his life, God holds Abraham up as an example of a giant in the faith for us to follow. In other words, his legacy speaks volumes concerning his walk with his God. That is exactly what God desires for us. God's desire for each of us is that our commitment to Him is more than just Sunday morning but that it is 24/7. God desires that we live with such a holy passion that every single moment of each day be totally committed to Him.

> **GOD DESIRES THAT WE LIVE WITH SUCH A HOLY PASSION THAT EVERY SINGLE MOMENT OF EACH DAY BE TOTALLY COMMITTED TO HIM.**

As we study the life of Abraham we must ask, "Why could God say that Abraham was His friend?" I asked that question and discovered there are three traits concerning Abraham's life that really stand out and they all deal with the spiritual anatomy of his relationship with God.

THE KEY OF THE LISTENING EAR

The first key to know about the listening ear is the *importance* of hearing. Abraham demonstrated that he had his ear tuned to God. When God looked at Abraham's life He knew that Abraham was zeroed in to listening to what God was saying. This is a key to Abraham's life that every Christian should learn and apply. It is important that we listen to our heavenly Father instead of spending all our time with Him telling Him what He's going to do for us.

A teacher approached his class one day and assisted them in making an observation about their physical anatomy. He said, "I want you to look around the class and take a close look at each other." Then he asked the class to focus on each other's face. As the class followed the professor's instructions the question was raised, "Do you see something unique?" Many answers came back from the students. Wanting to make his point the teacher drew this observation, "God made you with two ears and only one mouth." The obvious became a practical lesson. Could it be that God intends for us to listen more than we speak? A person who has the gift of gab will find this hard to do, but it is a wise thing to do. Most arguments or disagreements could be avoided if we would apply the simple art of listening more than speaking.

We need to learn how to listen to God. Do you know if you will learn how to listen to God, you will be amazed at what God will say to you? The promise of God's Word bears out this truth.

One day I was called upon to do a friend's funeral. He was over 50 years of age and at one time a faithful lay minister in our church. In recent years he had gone through some trials and tribulations that life has a tendency to bring. Sitting on the platform, I looked into the faces of his family, friends, and co-workers who had come to pay their respects to a man they cared for deeply. I was seeking the right passage of Scripture to share in hopes of alleviating their pain of loss. The Scripture which came to mind was Psalm 46. It reminds us that God is our refuge and strength, a very present help in our times of trouble. As you read this familiar passage, you come to a great command of God through the psalmist. He says, "Be still and know that I am God" (Psalm 46:10). In the midst of whatever we may be called upon to endure, we are to cease striving and spend time getting to know God.

Just knowing about God is not enough. We all know something about God. We must know Him and then listen to Him. Bill Bright once wrote concerning communicating with God through prayer, "God longs to meet with us in prayer because prayer represents the difference between truly knowing Him and merely knowing about Him."[1] If we would just stop long enough and listen, we would hear God speaking to us. He speaks to us through His Word, through ministers preaching His truth, and through other believers. There are times we must just draw aside and be still in order to hear His still small voice speaking to our souls.

Think with me for a moment. We are living in a fast-paced society and from time to time we need to cease the striving that we spend so much of our time doing and get with God. We need to learn how to take our energy and control it for a while, and to be zeroed in so that we can hear the very voice of God. If you can find a place of solitude away from all the activities of a busy life, you may be amazed at what the Father says about the issues of life. If you will be still and listen, you will hear that still, small voice shouting wisdom to your soul in an unmistakable tone. If you are having marital problems, He will be a wonderful Counselor to bring a healing balm to brokenness. He will speak to you about the marriage relationship and give you help with the challenges of the home. If single, God will speak to you about your singleness and how to deal with the challenges of singleness in our kind of society. Whatever the need, God has a word for you.

God will share wisdom concerning our marriage, our singleness, our career and especially our character. He speaks to us about our spiritual lives as well. He will instruct us about our salvation, our discipleship, as well as the stewardship of our lives if we will listen to Him. I am simply challenging you to a dynamic relationship with the One who loves you the most. It is a covenant relationship.

John Guest wrote an article in *Christianity Today* some time ago called "Only a Prayer Away." In the article he nails this kind of relationship with God. He writes...

> *"Just as a husband and a wife live out their lives against the backdrop of being married, so do we live out the entirety of our lives against the backdrop of a constant relationship with God. He is always there, always loving us, always ready to listen to us. As we recognize His unwavering commitment to us, we are able to live in the day to day adventure and challenges of His presence. It is as if we say, 'Oh, I must talk to him about this.'"* [2]

He is always there ready to make His presence and will known to us.

Recently I picked up a magazine that contained human interest stories about those whose lives have been greatly impacted by God. It shared a story about an Air Force pilot who was flying across a channel in war time when he lost his bearings and radio contact with his air base at a pivotal time of his mission. It was dangerous for him to try to make contact by radio due to fear that the enemy would be able to lock in on his position. Anxiety was high and even more so when he looked at his gauge and it showed that the plane was about to lose all its fuel. He was literally flying over the channel on a wing and a prayer. He said he began to perspire and was afraid of what was about to take place. After a period of time, he turned the radio back on and started fiddling with the dial to try to find a voice somewhere that could lead him safely home. As he moved around the dial, he finally heard a very faint voice that led him all the way back to safety. As I read that story I thought, "That is just like God." When we're going through struggles and the stress of living here on the face of the earth and we're twisting the dials of our life trying to find direction, if we will listen we can hear God say, "If you'll just be still, if you'll just listen, if you'll just turn your dial toward Me, I will lead you safely home." We need to learn the importance of hearing from God.

The second key about the listening ear is the *insightfulness* of hearing. When a person fine-tunes his hearing to God he discovers the ability to discern the true nature of the One speaking. When we focus our hearing to the sovereign Lord, we can discern what He is saying about all situations in our lives and be able to view them from His perspective. That is the desire of God's heart. Abraham demonstrated what later the prophet Jeremiah would teach...

> *Call to me and I will answer you and I will tell you great and mighty things which you do not know. (Jeremiah 33:3)*

What a promise from our heavenly Father!

Abraham sought the Lord and the Lord appeared to him and showed him great and mighty things. What God did for Abraham He still desires to do for us today. Do you know that when God appeared and spoke to Abraham it was an act of grace on the behalf of God? Abraham would not have been one I would have chosen if I were God to go speak to. Why? Because he was an idolater. He and his family worshiped other gods yet when Abraham heard God, something happened. It generated a believing faith in Abraham. Isn't that the way it happened in your life? You may not have known you were an idolater but before you ever came to Christ, I guarantee you were worshiping other things. However, when God spoke to you through the Gospel, it arrested your faith and you believed in the atoning work of Jesus. It was God's voice that brought you into believing faith. I like the way the writer of Hebrews says it. He says when Abraham was called, he obeyed. He had believing faith. From Genesis 12 to Genesis 25 you will find this phrase, "and the word of the Lord kept coming to Abraham...and Abraham kept believing God." So we need to see the importance of being still and listening and when we listen to God, He will give us spiritual discernment and insight.

The third key concerning the listening ear is the *impact* of hearing. When God speaks to your heart and you listen and obey, you discover it equals the blessings of God. There is an equation that must be followed. First, you hear God, then you obey God and it equals out to the blessings of God. Study the life of Abraham and you will see a principle at work that you can probably relate to. When he obeyed, he found blessing. When he acted apart from God, he found trouble.

Let's qualify this principle through Christian stewardship. It is one area of the Christian life which can easily demonstrate this teaching. The Scripture teaches that the believer is to practice storehouse tithing. We are to bring ten percent of our income to the church where we hold membership. Every Christian understands ten percent is the beginning point, yet seventy percent of those who attend church on Sunday do not tithe. Evangelist Bill Stafford states, "...the offering time in the worship service is the most disobedient moment of worship in the average church every Sunday." Follow through with me. The promise of Scripture is found in the Book of Malachi.

> Bring the whole tithe into the storehouse, so that there may be food in My house, and test me now in this," says the Lord of hosts, "if I will not open for you the windows of heaven, and pour out for you a blessing until it overflows." (Malachi 3:10)

This is basic Stewardship 101; however, the vast majority of Christians have read what God said and would proclaim it to be true, yet still choose to operate apart from God. In fact, they have the audacity to believe somehow God is going to make an exception for them. He, in their mind, is going to cast His Word aside and go against what He said. To believe such is just spiritual immaturity. His promise is – you bring the tithe, God will open

WHEN A CHRISTIAN CHOOSES TO DISOBEY ... HE HAS CHOSEN TO BYPASS THE BLESSINGS OF GOD.

up the windows of Heaven and pour out His blessings. To disobey is to get only what you can do for yourself. When a Christian chooses to disobey in this area, he has chosen to bypass the blessings of God. Any excuse you come up with as to why you have chosen not to tithe will sound acceptable. Satan will make sure of it, but I promise it doesn't make spiritual sense in the ears of God. You know why? Because of the formula. You hear God, you obey God, you do it God's way, and it equals to the blessings of God upon your life. Yet when

WHEN WE DO IT GOD'S WAY WHAT WE ARE DOING IS INVITING GOD TO DO HIS VERY BEST IN OUR LIVES.

you hear God and know what is true and you choose not to obey Him, then you erase the final conclusion of God's equation. God cannot bless you.

Max Lucado has a statement that I read and it was seared into my soul. It applies to every segment of the Christian life. He says, "When we do it God's way (as taught through His Word) what we are doing is inviting God to do His very best in our lives." Abraham's life bears witness of this principle. Because of his hearing and obedience, he became a blessing to every nation just as God had promised. It was a fulfillment of Scripture (Genesis 12:1-3). Therefore, God was able to make him an agent of blessing.

The principle can be found throughout Abraham's life.

HEARING GOD PLUS OBEYING GOD EQUALS THE BLESSINGS OF GOD.

Remember? Hearing God plus obeying God equals the blessings of God. Hearing God, then acting apart from God (disobeying Him) results in trouble. Let me give you just one example in the life of this friend of God. It is found in Genesis 16 where God told Abraham and Sarah that He was going to bless them with an offspring. They were at the twilight of their lives and could not even fathom how this could be. Hebrews shares their sentiment when it describes this event.

Abraham

Therefore, there was born of one man, and him as good as dead at that… (Hebrews 11:12)

Here they were, Abraham and Sarah, past childbearing time. Sarah thought it was so funny when she heard she was going to bear a child that she hid behind the flap of the tent and laughed. Sarah did something natural that many of us would have done. She failed to realize God was going to do something supernatural. He was going to provide a way for them to have a child. Instead of waiting on God, Sarah tried to help God along. She went to her maiden named Hagar and said to her, "God said I'm going to have a baby and I'm too old to have children, so why don't you go in and have relations with my husband and you bear the offspring?" This was not God's plan. Hagar did what Sarah asked and gave birth to a son named Ishmael. This act of disobedience has caused nothing but trouble even to this day. Much of the unrest in the Middle East can be traced back to this chapter in the Word of God. Abraham and Sarah acted apart from God and trouble followed. When I know God's will, when I know what God has said and I do not obey God, I, like Abraham, take myself out from the blessings of God. The same is true for you. The key to friendship with God is to have listening ears.

THE KEY OF OBEDIENT FEET

Let me give you a second key God gives concerning Abraham. The Scripture says not only did he have listening ears but Abraham also had obedient feet. Read what God says of Abraham.

Legacy

By faith Abraham, when he was called, obeyed
by going out to a place which he was to receive for an
inheritance... (Hebrews 11:8)

In Genesis 12:4 the Scripture states,

So Abram went forth as the Lord had spoken
to him; and Lot with him. Now Abram was seventy-
five years old when he departed from Haran.

Abraham had a heart to obey God so he set out on a faith journey with God. Yes, even at his age. Some that I know who are 70+ are just waiting to go to sleep one day and wake up in Heaven. Some say "I'm too old to start something new." However, the testimony of Abraham speaks volumes. At the age when so many are quitting, he was just at the beginning point of walking with God. He heard the call of God and responded with obedient feet.

There are two things I want you to note about obedient feet. First, take a close look at the actions of the *listener*. It is recorded of Abraham that he went forth as the Lord had spoken to him. His faith moved to action. The truth is simple. Faith with no action is no faith at all. The Christian life is one of hearing from God, then taking steps of obedience. It costs to hear God and it also costs to obey God. It costs to hear what God says. It causes one to focus on God. Once God speaks it will always cost to be obedient to Him. God said to Abraham, "Abraham, I want you to leave your country." It was a call to leave his comfort zone. He had lived in one area all his life, 70 years, and now he was asked to leave and trust God to show him a new land. God was calling him from home missions to foreign missions. It would demand great faith.

God moves it up a notch. "I want you to leave your family." Leaving your country is one thing but your family is quite another matter. It would demand greater faith. The older I become the importance of family increases. What was God up to? The Almighty was stripping away everything so Abraham would totally depend upon Him. "I want you to leave your father's household." No big deal, you say. No, we need to understand what this meant. For him to leave his father's house was to leave his inheritance. In our culture most live for their inheritance. People actually count the days until they receive their inheritance. I love the bumper sticker that says, "I'm spending my kids' inheritance!" I think my parents are doing just that and seem to be having a great time in their doing. Rightfully so. God said, "Abraham, leave your father's inheritance and I'm going to show you the land you're going to." Abraham did exactly what God asked of him, even when Abraham did not know exactly where he was going. Every day he focused on the promises of God… "I'm going to make you a great nation. I'm going to make your name great. Your family is going to be as numerous as the stars in heaven, as numerous as the grains of sand on the beach. Abraham, if you'll just follow me and obey me, I'm going to make your name great."

Have you ever considered what God was teaching us through Abraham? In order to gain the blessings of God he had to turn loose of something in his life. He had to turn loose

> **THE ALMIGHTY WAS STRIPPING AWAY EVERYTHING SO ABRAHAM WOULD TOTALLY DEPEND UPON HIM.**

of that which was familiar. Abraham had to turn loose of the family. He had to turn loose of that which was comfortable. He had to turn loose of his own desires in order to take on the blessings of God. Is this not true in our lives as well? Either

EITHER WE'RE GOING TO TURN LOOSE OF OUR OWN DESIRES IN ORDER TO TAKE HOLD OF THE BLESSINGS OF GOD, OR WE'RE GOING TO HOLD ON TO OUR DESIRES AND THEREFORE, FORFEIT THE BLESSINGS OF GOD.

we're going to turn loose of our own desires in order to take hold of the blessings of God, or we're going to hold on to our desires and therefore, forfeit the blessings of God. If you want to know how to be a friend of God, you have to have listening ears and then you have to have obedient feet. Your faith in God must move you to action.

Second, you need to see the actions of the *Lord*. God hears Abraham as he said "I'm going to follow God." He packs everything he owns, gets up and starts walking out of town. He lived in a tent which meant he was always ready to move for God. As he moved out with obedient feet, God did three things for Abraham, and He'll do the same for you.

GOD WILL MAKE SURE YOU SUCCEED IN FOLLOWING HIS WILL.

First, He brought all the *authority* of Heaven upon Abraham. As he obeyed, God brought the authority of Heaven upon his life. Pay close attention to the actions of the Lord. The Scripture is plain. It says in Luke 1:37, "For no word from God shall be void of power." So when God speaks to you and calls you to greater obedience which demands steps of faith and you obey His leading, all of Heaven's power will be upon you. When you listen and obey, He enables, empowers, and blesses you. God will make sure you succeed in following His will.

Second, obedience to God will always bring the *arrangements* of Heaven upon your life. God paints in broad strokes across the canvas of your life. He shows you the big picture. As you follow, He fills in all the little details to flesh out His perfect plan.

Let me illustrate. In 1980, God called me to pastor North Metro First Baptist Church. I could tell you exactly the will of God, the vision God gave me. He said, "I want you to build and grow one of the great spiritual feeding stations in Gwinnett County that will touch the world." That distinct vision God gave me continues to be the big picture to this very day; however, day by day He continues to reveal the details, the next step, in His master plan. I am so glad that's the way it happens. If He had shown me all the details of everything I was going to have to go through in order to try to fulfill the vision He gave me, I probably would have said, "No, God, not me, get someone else." As I've taken each step of faith, God paints more strokes on the canvas as His will is being accomplished. He reveals to me at every juncture what He wants me to accomplish next. It is a walk of faith. With each step He arranges all of Heaven to see that I accomplish His will. One must walk by faith.

As you obey, there is the third blessing God will bring to you. He will also bring into your life the *abundance* of Heaven. In other words, God's children will never have to beg. God's children will never have to worry that whatever He asks of you He will make sure all the abundance of Heaven is upon your life. For salvation, let me tell you what He will do. He will seal you for the day of redemption. For those who struggle with tithing, if you will just take the steps of obedience and begin to tithe, God will arrange all of Heaven to meet every need you have materially and financially. If you are dealing with direction in your life, He will navigate you and lead you to your destination. The faith walk is the greatest walk anyone could be called to live. Henry Blackaby states it well, "Strong—growing—God-sized faith begins with a simple step of obedience based on all we know of God." Let me ask a penetrating question: What do you know of God? The answers are plentiful, but let me give you two that are trustworthy. What you know of God can be boiled down to two things. He is faithful and He can be trusted. God's friend has obedient feet. That leads me to the last key about being a friend of God.

> **STRONG, (GROWING) GOD-SIZED FAITH BEGINS WITH A SIMPLE STEP OF OBEDIENCE BASED ON ALL WE KNOW OF GOD.**

THE KEY OF THE STEADY EYE

You have to have steady eyes. Notice this about Abraham. He was focused on two things. First, the goal. In Hebrews 11:10 it tells us,

> *He was looking for the city which has foundations, whose architect and builder is God."*

Think with me about the two words, "the city." The city is Heaven. Abraham knew instinctively by faith that there was a Heaven and there was a city of God and he was pointing toward Heaven in every action he took.

Abraham

Someone asked how in the world did Abraham know about the city of Heaven? Oliver Green, an old independent Baptist preacher now in Heaven said this, "The same way Abel knew about the blood sacrifice and Noah knew that the flood was coming, God spoke to Abraham and told him about the city." He was focused on the city and in everything he did, he wanted to bring honor and glory to God. The same should be true of you. You should have a desire to bring honor and glory to God through the obedient walk of faith.

Second, he not only focused on the goal but he focused on God. He wanted to honor God. Do you want to honor God? You see, he had one desire and that was doing the Master's will.

Not long ago I arrived home and was tired. I had just come off eight weeks of constant going and I was fatigued. I took my leisure on the sofa in our den, took the remote control and began to flip through the TV stations. There was nothing good on TV that night and I went to MSNBC and there was an image of President Bush going around the White House. Brit Hume was interviewing him as they were walking on the White House lawn. As they were making the transition from the White House lawn into the Oval Office, the President was asked a loaded question. The reporter asked, "Mr. President, we recognize your faith is very important to you." Bush said, "Oh yes, it's everything to me. I pray all the time. I pray in the morning before I get out of bed. I pray in the shower. I pray while getting dressed. When I'm walking over to the Oval Office, I pray. Even when I come into the Oval Office, all day long there are several times during the day that I'll pause and pray."[3] As they walked into the Oval Office, the camera scanned up at this portrait of a man on a horse charging up a hill. The caption read, *A Charge to Keep*. Hume asked, "There must be something significant about this picture for you to hang it here in the Oval Office." President Bush looked in that boyish way and said, "Oh yes, it's part of my faith. It's kind of like the Methodist hymn by the same title, *A Charge to Keep*." Then the quote came, "A charge to keep I have, a God to glorify, a never-dying soul to save and fit it for the sky. To serve the present age, my calling to fulfill, O may it all my powers engage to do my Master's will."[4]

In a day where so many are trying to secularize our society, I listened to our President say he wanted to fulfill his Master's will. It doesn't matter if you're a politician, an attorney, a doctor, or a postal worker who delivers the mail. It does not matter if all you do is ride on the back of a garbage truck or are a Baptist preacher. The same is true for everyone. In everything you do, listen to God, obey God, and it equals the blessings of God. At the end of your life God will say "Oh, he was my friend!"

5

DAVID:
A MAN AFTER GOD'S HEART

Your choices today – determine your lifestyle tomorrow!
Ike Reighard

*P*aul was at Antioch and on the Sabbath Day he went to the Synagogue as was his custom. While there the Synagogue officials insisted for the Apostle Paul to bring an exhortation. Paul stood and held his hands high quieting the crowd and said...

"Men of Israel, and you who fear God, listen: The God of this people Israel chose our fathers, and made the people great during their stay in the land of Egypt, and with an uplifted arm He led them out from it. And for a period of about forty years He put up with them in the wilderness. When He had destroyed seven nations in the land of Canaan, He distributed their land as an inheritance—all of which took about four hundred and fifty years. And after these things He gave them judges until Samuel the prophet. Then they asked for a king, and God gave them Saul the son of Kish, a man of the tribe of Benjamin, for forty years. And after He had removed him, He raised up David to be their king, concerning whom He also testified and said, 'I HAVE FOUND DAVID the son of Jesse, A MAN AFTER MY HEART, who will do all My will.'" (Acts 13:16-23)

Legacy

Please remember we're talking about building a legacy of our lives which in turn brings honor and glory to God. David was one of those special ones God chose to lay his life out before us. It is like God says, "I want to tell you about this one's life." Then God ascribes to David one of the highest legacies anyone could hope to be said about them.

> *I have found David the son of Jesse, a man after My own heart, who will do all My will. (Acts 13:22)*

When you come to the Scriptures you will find that God says some powerful things about different people. We have discovered…. it has been said that Noah found favor; it has been said that Abraham was a friend of God. God now says that David was "a man after My own heart."

There is probably no greater name in all the world history of names, next to Jesus Christ, than the name of King David. When you ask people what biblical names stand out to them, they will inevitably bring up the name of David. Then probing further as to what they know about David, you will be amazed as to what they do know. First, they know of his greatest *triumph*, and second they know of his greatest *tragedy*. We would be wise to study both of these and gain wisdom from the triumph and from the tragedy of David's life.

The greatest triumph of David took place in the valley of Elah. It was there King Saul and the army of Israel was camped on one hillside and the Philistine army was on the other. The only physical barrier between these two great armies was the valley of Elah. In the center of this valley would be the very place where God would begin to raise up

David to prominence. It would be the site of David's greatest victory. The victory came when David slew the giant Goliath. Believe me, this was a day of tremendous celebration. Israel had a new hero and his name was David, the boy who would become king.

In this same young man, like so many of us, was the potential for failure as well. The power of great triumph is what we all strive for but on the heels of victory hovers the opportunity for tragedy. So it was in David's life. It is worthy of our study because some who are reading this are facing defeat because of sin. The great tragedy you may be facing may be the same as David's. Some have felt the sting of adultery and its devastating affects. We need to learn from David and glean the lessons. If we do, it will cause us to be wise in our walk with God.

There are three things I want you to see in the life of David.

THE MAN AND HIS FAITH

The first is what I call the man and his faith. I want you to see how David's faith brought triumph to David's life. In my study of David, I discovered four things that naturally jump out about his faith walk with God. Remember God said, here was a man who was "after My own heart." Well, if David was that man, we need to learn what it was that set David apart.

First, David lived a life of *trust*. He understood the importance of trusting God. A student of the Book of Psalms will discover a young shepherd and later a king who demonstrated great faith in his God. It wasn't a matter of circumstances in his life; it was a matter of confidence this young shepherd boy had in his Creator to see him through whatever life hurled his way. David knew that God would be faithful to him. How we need to learn this from David's life. All of us have circumstances we would not choose. Like David, we can trust His heart.

When journeying through God's Hall of Fame, one discovers those whom God uses the most seem to go through a period of learning to trust Him. I have read of great men of God who at the height of their ministries seemed to go through a time of brokenness that built their trust.

One such man was Charles Haddon Spurgeon of England. In the greatest days of his ministry, he would come home from a hard day of ministry caring for his flock to a bedridden wife. As he ministered to his ailing wife, he considered the truth of the promises of God. One night sitting by her bed with only the light from the fire, he penned his trust of God.

> *God is too good to be unkind. He is too wise*
> *to be mistaken. When you cannot trace His hand,*
> *you can always trust His heart.* [1]

There were times in David's life when he too had learned that no matter what the circumstances, he could always trust the heart of God.

David not only lived a life of trust, he was also living a life of *worship*! I serve as chaplain of the Collins Hill High School football team. One night we were playing a cross-town rival. Just to be honest Collins Hill was hitting on all cylinders scoring at will. One of the players came over to me and said, "Pastor, isn't it strangely quiet out here tonight?" I listened and with all the excitement of what was going on in that game, it seemed like it was strangely quiet considering there were thousands of spectators in the stands watching the game. When they should have been screaming, shouting and rejoicing they were quiet. It was surreal.

I feel that describes church on an average Sunday. You walk into the house of God, the congregation is singing the great songs of the faith, the orchestra and choir are doing their best, the man of God stands up and delivers the message and the people, who you think would break out in praise and worship, just sit there. It is confusing at times. The people of God come to the place of God to give praise to God, yet remain quiet. David was a man who understood what worship was all about. His whole life was built on faith. He had experienced God first hand and all he could do was explode in true worship.

In Psalm 8, you will find one of the greatest texts of Scripture written by David as he was worshiping God. One needs to understand something about David in his worship of his Creator. It created three vibrant things in his life.

As he worshiped it created an *atmosphere of awe* toward God. David knew God as the Creator of this universe and he wanted God to know how he viewed Him. David cries out in praise....

> *O Lord, our Lord, How majestic is Thy name in all the earth, Who hast displayed Thy splendor above the heavens!* ² *From the mouth of infants and nursing babes Thou hast established strength, Because of Thine adversaries, To make the enemy and the revengeful cease. (Psalms 8:1-2)*

And then in verse 3 he says,

> *When I consider Your heavens, the work of Your fingers, The moon and the stars, which You have ordained, ⁴What is man that You are mindful of him? (Psalms 8:3-4)*

When we think of David going out at night we only think of the night he looked down from the king's palace roof and saw Bathsheba. However, there was another time that he went out at night and looked up into the sky. He saw the moon and the stars. He saw the handiwork of God in creation and it generated praise and worship. Do you know what I have discovered about David? He slowed down enough to meditate upon God. David paused long enough to look around and see the work of God and to contemplate what God desired to do in David's life.

A few years ago my wife and I were facing one of the biggest decisions of our lives. We went down to a place where we love to get alone and rest. We knew in order to make the enormous decision we were being asked to make, we needed to be in a place where we could hear God. The place we rented that week was overlooking the ocean. Day after day we wrestled with the decision before us. On one particular night we were weary from processing this decision to the point we could not sleep. At two o'clock in the morning we found ourselves sitting out on a patio watching the wave's crash on the beach below. It was the time of year when it seemed like the moon had just settled down within arms reach. I had always heard about the man in the moon as a child, but on this night we could literally reach up and touch his face. The sky was extremely clear. It was as though the heavens were the sanctuary of God. We felt the presence of God and we worshipped Him. The Almighty taught us that we could trust the One who had strategically placed every star in place and hung the moon in the sky. Both Mary and I sat back and knew we could trust God with everything in our lives including this decision.

It was the same kind of night that David looked up and realized he could trust God with everything. When he looked around and saw the handiwork of God, it produced a great fulfillment and joy in him. Praise and worship flowed forth from his humble heart. The greatest need that we have in our fast-paced society is just simply to slow down and focus on God and consider Him in all of His majesty and glory. As we meditate upon His majesty we, like David, will stand in awe. It will literally change our worship. We will walk into the sanctuary full of praise. If He is who the Scriptures say He is, then we can know He will be faithful to us. This will generate a life of trust and worship! He had great awe of God.

David not only stood in awe of God, he had great *abandonment* to God that stemmed from a life of faith, trust and worship. In Psalm 8:4 he says...

> *What is man that You are mindful of him,*
> *And the son of man that You visit him? (Psalms*
> *8:4)*

David spent a life of intimacy with God. He walked with Him and talked with Him. He would spend time out in the shepherd's fields listening for the voice of his wonderful God. In the stillness of the moment he wrote about God. When you read from the pen of the shepherd boy there is one thing you can count on. David knew he could totally surrender to God and that God was concerned about every care David had in his life.

Total surrender builds trust into everyday life. A dear lady in our community is going through extreme medical problems. Her life at this stage is occupied by doctors, hospitals and for sure a great deal of anxiety. A few days ago she shared about her journey and also how she tried to relieve some of the stress. Often after a doctor's visit she would go to the YMCA and swim laps. One particular afternoon she made her way to the "Y" for some stress relief. She was about to encounter God in a visual way or at least in a way where God wanted to give her a gentle reminder of Psalm 8:4. A young father came in with his small baby that looked to be about one year old. They went to the deep end of the pool and with the baby secured in the father's arms, the young father took a leap into the pool. She said, "I watched as they emerged from underneath the water. Both were spitting out water and gasping for air." With peace springing forth she made this observation. "I realized that no matter what I am called to go through, no matter how deep the waters may be, I am confident that God always wraps His arms around me and sees me through. I can trust Him no matter what I'm faced with in my life."

David understood the principle this dear lady had come to grasp, that no matter the deep waters he might have to go through, God wraps His loving arms around him and cares for every concern David would face. The same is true for you. With all confidence you can, by faith, rest in great abandonment to God.

Quickly notice a third thing about David's worship of

David

God. It not only gave him great awe of God and abandonment to serve God, but David also had a desire to take great *action* for God. David had one thing that was burning brightly in his heart. He wanted to do something tremendous for God. He wanted to have high impact for his heavenly Father. Such a desire flows from a life of trust, worship and faith. David had all three in his walk with God. Trust came from knowing God personally and knowing you could count on His word as truth. Whatever God says in His word one must trust He can bring it to pass. He is Sovereign God. Worship follows as we adore our great Creator for all His majestic attributes. We trust and worship. However, if you desire to have maximum impact, you must take steps of faith which means to become obedient to God who has so ordered your steps.

> ... TO HAVE MAXIMUM IMPACT YOU MUST TAKE STEPS OF FAITH WHICH MEANS TO BECOME OBEDIENT TO GOD WHO HAS SO ORDERED YOUR STEPS.

David was such a man; therefore, it invited God's *favor* upon his life. A life that trusts and worships God will come to the point of obeying Him. When you obey, it will invite the favor of God upon your life. Let me allow David's life to illustrate such a point. Can you remember when David burst on the scene? It was when his father asked him to run an errand.

> *Now David was the son of the Ephrathite of Bethlehem in Judah, whose name was Jesse, and he had eight sons. And Jesse was old in the days of Saul, advanced in years among men. And the three older sons of Jesse had gone after Saul to the battle. And the names*

of his three sons who went to the battle were Eliab
the first-born, and the second to him Abinadab, and
the third Shammah. And David was the youngest.
Now the three oldest followed Saul, but David went
back and forth from Saul to tend his father's flock at
Bethlehem. And the Philistine came forward morning
and evening for forty days, and took his stand.

Then Jesse said to David his son, "Take now for
your brothers an ephah of this roasted grain and these
ten loaves, and run to the camp to your brothers.
Bring also these ten cuts of cheese to the commander
of their thousand, and look into the welfare of your
brothers, and bring back news of them. For Saul and
they and all the men of Israel are in the valley of Elah,
fighting with the Philistines." (1 Samuel 17:12-19)

Now the errand David's father, Jesse, asked him to
run was a simple one. It was more than loaves of bread and
blocks of cheese. God was orchestrating young David's life to
be a mighty instrument for God's purpose. Evidently this was
a trip which David had made many times. However, on this
trip God was going to prove Himself in a great way to this
young shepherd boy and also to Israel.

When David arrived in the camp of the army of Israel,
he noticed something strange about the army of King Saul.
As he stood on the hillside he saw the mighty army standing
there full of fear. In fact they were paralyzed by their fear.
Down in the valley, a giant by the name of Goliath had made
a regular practice of coming out and taunting the army of
God.

David

And he stood and shouted to the ranks of Israel, and said to them, "Why do you come out to draw up in battle array? Am I not the Philistine and you servants of Saul? Choose a man for yourselves and let him come down to me. If he is able to fight with me and kill me, then we will become your servants; but if I prevail against him and kill him, then you shall become our servants and serve us." Again the Philistine said, "I defy the ranks of Israel this day; give me a man that we may fight together." When Saul and all Israel heard these words of the Philistine, they were dismayed and greatly afraid. (1 Samuel 17:8-11)

I have read this story hundreds of times over the years. Every time, I come away with one strong impression. There was something different about David in comparison to the men in the army of Israel and different from their leader King Saul. The king and his army were paralyzed by their fear but young David was propelled by his faith. What a major difference. The same is true of so many Christians today. Many are afraid to take great steps of faith. God may be calling you forth to take a mighty stand for His kingdom, but fear, not faith, has captured your life. Fear has convinced you that you will find ways to blow it so don't even try. If you are not careful you will cower down. The army of Israel stood there on that hillside like cowards all because of fear.

> **THE KING AND HIS ARMY WERE PARALYZED BY THEIR FEAR BUT YOUNG DAVID WAS PROPELLED BY HIS FAITH.**

What was the major difference? Let me state the obvious. The army of Israel was taunted by Goliath, but David was trained by God and that, my friend, is the big difference. All the way through David's young life God was preparing him for this moment in time. Do you know the same is true for you? God has been working in your life in ways that you would think insignificant. Yet, from David we learn everything God does for you in the little insignificant things is preparing you for the Big Event in your life. There will be a moment when all the little lessons come together for the big God-size step of faith in making a great impact for God. The greatness of God in the small obscure places instills within one's life a faith that God is faithful and can be trusted.

THE GREATNESS OF GOD IN THE SMALL OBSCURE PLACES INSTILLS WITHIN ONE'S LIFE A FAITH THAT GOD IS FAITHFUL AND CAN BE TRUSTED.

The story continues with Goliath challenging the Israelites, "Send out just one man. If he defeats me, the Philistines will serve you, but if I defeat him then Israel will become our servants and serve us." (I Samuel 17:9) David, with the spunk of a shepherd boy, turned to see who was rising up to go take care of this giant. To his astonishment he saw nothing but fear, not faith. Here they were the mighty army of Israel, a.k.a. the mighty army of God, full of fear. Even Saul, their great leader, tried to bribe someone into going.

When all the men of Israel saw the man, they fled from him and were greatly afraid. And the men of Israel said, "Have you seen this man who is coming up? Surely he is coming up to defy Israel. And it will be that the king will enrich the man who kills him with great riches and will give him his daughter and make his father's house free in Israel." (1 Samuel 17:24-25)

Still no man would answer the challenge. David probably thought, "I can't believe you men. Are you not the army of the Lord? Look how fearful you are." Can you relate to this story? With so many victories to be won in our day, I fear God looks at us, the soldiers of the cross, and must be concerned with our trembling behind the doors of the churches.

David steps up and announces, "I'll go!" When God summons you into the battle there will always be someone of significance that will try to talk you out of obeying God. For David it was King Saul. The very one who should have been in the valley taking on this giant now was trying to talk David out of obedience. Why? Because his life was full of fear. Fear in Saul's life was trying to forfeit David from being used by God. The most fulfilling time in a person's life is when they know they are on mission for God. Saul said, "You are nothing but a youth!"

WHEN GOD SUMMONS YOU INTO THE BATTLE THERE WILL ALWAYS BE SOMEONE OF SIGNIFICANCE THAT WILL TRY TO TALK YOU OUT OF OBEYING GOD.

Then Saul said to David, "You are not able to go against this Philistine to fight with him; for you are but a youth while he has been a warrior from his youth." (1 Samuel 17:33)

When I first read this, I immediately saw the modern

church. I see adults afraid to engage the culture for the cause of Christ. Yet, when our youth believe what the adults teach them about doing the will of God, so many of those same adults give them numerous reasons why they should not obey.

David looked at Saul and rehearsed before him how God had prepared him for a time such as this.

> But David said to Saul, "Your servant was tending his father's sheep. When a lion or a bear came and took a lamb from the flock, I went out after him and attacked him, and rescued it from his mouth; and when he rose up against me, I seized him by his beard and struck him and killed him. Your servant has killed both the lion and the bear; and this uncircumcised Philistine will be like one of them, since he has taunted the armies of the living God." And David said, "The LORD who delivered me from the paw of the lion and from the paw of the bear, He will deliver me from the hand of this Philistine." And Saul said to David, "Go, and may the LORD be with you." (1 Samuel 17:34-37)

What a message! I can just hear David addressing the mighty king. "Saul, God not only protected me, He also delivered me!" Faith was real and alive to David. He knew he could trust the God of Israel and that God would see him through. Do you know how the king responded? "Better you than me. Go and may the Lord be with you."

Saul evidently did not know God like the shepherd boy David. David expressed a wonderful dynamic faith in

David

God that came from an ever increasing relationship. Because of such a faith, David went with the favor of God on him as he went out to meet Goliath. That is a goal every believer should seek in their walk with God. We should strive every day to operate in the favor of God. It all begins with our faith!

There are two aspects of David's faith we must examine. First, he had an *uncompromising faith*. Whatever God placed before him to accomplish in his mind, it was a done deal. He knew God would deliver him. It had been that way in the past and would be that way now against such a giant. The men of war gave him no chance against such an experienced warrior like Goliath, but God would prove to be more than capable to meet such a challenge.

As David was about to leave to go to battle, Saul cried out, "Wait a minute here, you can't go out there without armor. Take mine." Saul tried to weight him down with all his armor. Do you know this is the world's way? We'll get a direction from God and many will allow the world to turn them aside from doing God's will God's way. God has prepared us all of our lives to do His will a certain way and if we are not careful, we will listen to others try to get us to do it their way. If David had gone in the armor of Saul, he would never have defeated the giant. The boy who would become king had uncompromising faith that God had prepared and equipped him for the battle. He knew it would be the same as it was with the lion and the bear. He was trained, equipped and readied by the One who would strengthen and sustain him. He had to do it God's way, and he was not about to allow Saul, as well intentioned as he was, to turn him aside. Uncompromising faith is simply doing it God's way and relying upon God for the results. Through his tremendous faith David knew the

secret to life's challenges, "The battle belongs to the Lord!"
I hope you have learned that marvelous lesson in life. The

UNCOMPROMISING FAITH IS SIMPLY DOING IT GOD'S WAY AND RELYING UPON GOD FOR THE RESULTS.

battle always belongs to the Lord, and
he will see you through no matter what
the battle is.

So he gathered up his sling and
headed out to the valley of Elah. As
he crossed over the brook, he reached
down and picked up five smooth
stones. With uncompromising faith he was ready for Goliath
the Philistine.

There is another aspect of his faith that we need to learn
from David. When you study the life of David you discover
he had *unselfish faith.* David draws up close to Goliath and
gets engrossed in conversation. Goliath says, "Man, what is
this that they sent out a little punk to face me. I'm going to rip
you apart. Then I am going to feed your body to the foul of
the air." David looked at him and said, "Hey, the battle is the
Lord's! I want you to know that God is going to show today
that God is God and I will defeat you." I want you to see the
unselfish faith of David.

> Then David said to the Philistine, "You come to me
> with a sword, a spear, and a javelin, but I come to
> you in the name of the LORD of hosts, the God of
> the armies of Israel, whom you have taunted. This
> day the LORD will deliver you up into my hands,
> and I will strike you down and remove your head
> from you. And I will give the dead bodies of the army
> of the Philistines this day to the birds of the sky and
> the wild beasts of the earth, that all the earth may

know that there is a God in Israel, and that all this assembly may know that the LORD does not deliver by sword or by spear; for the battle is the LORD's and He will give you into our hands." (1 Samuel 17:45-47)

David is saying, "Hey Goliath! I want you to know today's your day! I'm going to sting you right between the eyes and I'm going to cut your head off, but I want you to know all the honor and all the glory belong to God!" Here's the heart that follows God. A person who is after God's own heart is willing to do God's will through faith and gives all the praise to Him. After David killed Goliath all the accolades were there, but David gave honor to God. God can and will use anyone who will bring all the glory to Him. Years ago a sweet lady by the name of Corrie ten Boom shared that kind of character toward God. She and her family hid Jews back in Nazi Germany. Later she received great recognition for all that she and her family did during that dangerous time in world history. One night someone asked her how she handled all the accolades she was receiving. She said, "At the end of the day I take all that has been said and turn them into a bouquet and give them to God who deserves all the glory." David was a man of great faith.

> **GOD CAN AND WILL USE ANYONE WHO WILL BRING ALL THE GLORY TO HIM.**

THE MAN AND HIS FAILURE

One cannot speak of David's tremendous faith without also seeing his failure. It's not enough just to see the greatest triumph in David's life. You have to see the greatest tragedy in David's life because most of us will be able to relate more to the tragedy than to the triumph. It is a fascinating story.

I want you to see three things concerning his failure. First, it is the same old *problem*. The problem plagued David as it plagues many who read this book. Fast forward -- David now is king of Israel. God has been faithful to His Word. God had anointed him as king through the prophet Samuel and in time would place him on the throne. He had to be patient while God cleared Saul off the throne. God did, and faithful to His word, installed David as the king. God wanted a man ruling over Israel whose heart was stayed on Him. David was such a man. Saul was not pursuing God, nor did he have a passion for God. David, on the other hand, lived a life of faith. From early on in his life he developed a love relationship with God. He worshipped him daily and honored Him with an obedient life. The result was the favor of God. The story of his life up to this point was ideal.

Then in II Samuel 11 we read some of the most tragic words found in God's word. Listen to them. "Then it happened." We all can relate to those three words. One day we are walking with God, everything is going well – "Then it happened!" Whatever "it" is may be different for each of us but we all know what "it" is for us. For David it was so tragic.

There came a time in the spring each year that all the kings of the nations led their armies out into battle. David, the man after God's own heart, for whatever reason, chose to stay behind in Jerusalem at the king's palace. Instead of being where he was suppose to be, he was out of pocket. Isn't that the way it usually happens? I, like you, have discovered that is a formula for trouble. My parents always drilled that same

David

truth into me growing up. The newscast of our day reminds us of this daily. When you're out of pocket, you always seem to be doing things you shouldn't be doing. We saw that in Gwinnett County, Georgia recently through a tragic accident involving three young students. One of the girls who didn't have her driver's license, was out of pocket, doing some things she shouldn't have been doing. She and two of her girlfriends were riding in a car they had stolen from one of their parents when they were tragically hit and instantly killed. Some of you right now are out of pocket, not doing it God's way. You are not living the way God wants you to live and you are reading this thinking you can get by with it. I want you to know when you're out of pocket, out of the will of God, tragedy has a way of finding your address. The Bible says the kings were out at battle but David chose to stay behind.

... WHEN YOU'RE OUT OF POCKET, OUT OF THE WILL OF GOD, TRAGEDY HAS A WAY OF FINDING YOUR ADDRESS.

The tragedy for King David begins. David couldn't sleep and there was probably some feeling in his soul that said, "I ought to be out there on the battlefield." His soul was restless. He walked out on his rooftop of the king's palace and looked down over Jerusalem. As the moon sparkled that night, it reflected upon a young lady who was bathing on her rooftop. You know the story; David's look turned into lust, his lust turned into adultery, and his adultery turned into devastation.

I want you to read this very carefully. I want you that have been there not to hear what I am about to say as condemnation or being judgmental. I have never met anyone yet who has had their look turn to lust and their lust turn to

87

adultery that would stand and testify it was one of the greatest things that ever happened to them in their lives. I have found just the opposite to be true. I've talked with hundreds who have been caught in that sin who have said, "It was the most devastating thing to my life."

Here was David, out of pocket, doing what he shouldn't have been doing, and his lust led him to say, "Go bring her to me." They brought Bathsheba to him and he said, "Who is she? Is this not the wife of Uriah?" At this point, David, the man after God's own heart, should have stopped. Instead David said, "Bring her to me" and the Bible says they had relations. David thought he had pulled it off, gotten away with it. Then he received the stunning news. Bathsheba sent word to the king, "I am pregnant!" Talk about devastation. He thought he had gotten by with the misstep. Nobody noticed. Nobody knew. Isn't that the way we think sometimes? Then out of the blue, "I'm pregnant." Well, David sat there and here is what he did. He began to learn something about sin. Sin always takes you further than you wanted to go, it always keeps you longer than you wanted to stay, and it always costs you more than you wanted to pay when you want out. David's heart which had been so tender toward God, now begins to harden.

He began to think how he could overcome this. The same old problem is sin and David reacts the same way we react. He said, "I'll cover it up." He called for Uriah, brought him home and said, "Go home and spend the night with your wife." He thought that would cover it up. I want you to read very carefully. Unlike David, Uriah remembered who his loyalty was pledged to, his king! He took his oath very seriously. He would always be faithful to his king, unlike David. Uriah, instead of going home, slept in the king's palace.

David

David found out and the next day he goes and has a little party with Uriah and gets him drunk and says, "Now go home" and Uriah, even in his drunken stupor, stayed faithful to his king to whom he had pledged his loyalty. The next day King David was seething with anger, wrote a note and gave it to Uriah and said, "Take this to Joab in the field." The note read, "Joab, when you get in the heat of the battle, I want you to pull all the troops back so Uriah will be killed." Notice what sin does to a person. His look turned to lust. Lust turned to adultery and now the results of adultery turned to murder. The word came back that Uriah was dead and then the Scripture says there was a time of mourning.

In II Samuel 11:27 we read words that demonstrate a hard heart. They will chill your bones. "And when the time of mourning was over, David sent and brought her to his house and she became his wife and then she bore him a son." If that's not tragic enough, you need to learn how to read the Word of God. There are some little words God strategically places in Scripture that are there to wake you up in order to rattle your cage and bring you back into reality. In this case the word is "but". The scripture says, "but" the time of mourning was over. He brought Bathsheba to his house, he married her, she bore him a son, and then you read ..."but". Be sure to read what follows.

But the thing that David had done was evil in the sight of the Lord. (II Samuel 11:27)

Covered up! But it was still evil in the sight of the Lord. It is not my sight you have to worry about. Your sight is not what I have to worry about. It is the sight of the Lord that we need to be concerned about. His vision is 20-20! It says, "But this thing he had done was evil in the sight of God." How tragic!

The second truth concerning his failure is the same old *principle*. Whatever you sow, you're going to reap. David had become slack in the basic disciplines of his life and gave Satan an entrance. Satan always works overtime to take you and me down. He is not in a hurry to take you out. He will let those little seeds of mischievousness, of lust, take root in your heart. All he knows is one day he is going to lead you to the place of destruction. He is not in a hurry. We have been warned many times in the Scripture. James tells us that when we give ourselves over to lust, "Lust is conceived and gives birth to sin and when sin is accomplished, it brings forth death." (James 1:15) The principle is there. Whatever you sow, you will reap.

Then there is a third truth to grasp. It is the same old *penalty*. It brings death to our fervency with God. Our passion for God grows cold. In II Samuel 12 God says, "Okay David, I love you too much to let you lie in your sin. I am going to deal with you about your sin." If you are His child, God loves you too much to let you stay in your sin. God shows He hates sin so much that wherever He finds it among His people, He will not let it go unchecked and if need be unpunished.

IF YOU ARE HIS CHILD, GOD LOVES YOU TOO MUCH TO LET YOU STAY IN YOUR SIN.

So God begins to deal with the king. I want you to know that a year has passed since the sin had taken place. God sent a prophet, a man of God to David by the name of Nathan. Nathan says, "David, I need to tell you a story" and David says, "Alright." Now Nathan is about to blow everything wide open. "David, let me tell you about what's happened in the kingdom." And David says, "What is it?" And he says "Well, there was a particular man who came into the backyard of another man and chose to take a little lamb, a defenseless lamb, that belonged to the other man. He stole it! David, I want you to know what happened. This man took that other man's little lamb and took it as his own and stole it from the man." And Scripture says that David began to seethe with anger and said, "You tell me who the man is! He must pay! I'll make sure he pays!" Nathan looked at David and said, "David, you are the man."

David's heart had grown so cold that when God spoke to him he could not even hear Him. When your heart grows so cold in your sin, that is when God is going to unveil it. You must always, always, always keep your heart tender toward God. You must always be willing when God points out a sin in your life to be quick to confess it. Why? Because what you cover up, God will uncover and what you uncover in confession, God will cover with His Son's blood. So now David seethed in anger and said, "Who is the man? He'll pay for this!" And Nathan said, "You are the man, David!" God is arresting David's soul and gaining his total attention. "David was it not enough that I made you king? Was it not enough that I gave you houses? Was it not enough that I gave you wives? Was it not enough that I supplied every need that you had? If that was not enough, David, I, God, would have given you more!" (II Samuel 12:7-9). God is not through. "Why have you despised the Word of the Lord by doing evil in His sight? You struck down Uriah. You killed a man all because of your sin, David." Conviction has settled in David's heart. Is God through with David? Read on!

THE MAN AND HIS FUTURE

As the story continues to unfold you have seen David in his triumph and now you have seen King David in his tragedy. The sin of adultery has led to devastation in the king's life. It is not just the sin of adultery; it is any sin that is not dealt with in a person's life.

Let us not stop at this point in David's life. I want you to see the man and his future because some of you right now are sitting there saying, "Boy, Frank, I'm there!" Oh, it may not be adultery, it may just be gossip. Sin is sin! It may not be adultery, it may not be murder, but it just may be that you stole something at work. So you say, "Am I through? Can God ever use me again?" Look at the man and his future.

David is at the point of *decision*. David knew he needed to make it right with God. So he confessed his sin out of a broken heart. In Psalm 51 it is evident that David no longer passes the buck. That is what sin causes you to do. "God, it's that wife you gave me! It's those kids who are rebelling. God! Hey, God, it's for this reason I went and did what I did." No, no, no! You just take responsibility. David quit passing the buck and cried out, "I've sinned against You, God! Against You only have I sinned and done evil in Your sight so You are justified when you speak and you're blameless when you judge" (Psalm 51:4). David calls for cleansing, "Wash me. Purify me. Create a clean heart in me" (Psalm 51:2,7,10). "Give me your presence. Sustain me with a willing spirit" (Psalm 51:11-12). Do you know what that means? It means a constant spirit not willing to yield to temptation again. "Give that to me, God!"

David comes to a point not only of decision but also a point of *dedication.* He cries out of conviction about his sin.

David

He cries for the compassion of God upon his sin. He cried out for communion with his sovereign God (Psalm 51:9-19), and David dedicated his life for a restored relationship with God.

What does it mean to be a man after God's own heart? It is quite simple. It is focusing on God, allowing Him to shape your life daily. In the small things you allow God, through your faithfulness, to prepare you for the point of maximum impact. Believe me, He is preparing you just as He did in David's life as a shepherd. God raised him up to defeat Goliath.

> **IN THE SMALL THINGS YOU ALLOW GOD, THROUGH YOUR FAITHFULNESS, TO PREPARE YOU FOR THE POINT OF MAXIMUM IMPACT.**

It also means you are not perfect. I used to get confused as David was heralded as a man after God's own heart. I could not get passed David and Bathsheba. How could someone who was passionate about their relationship with God commit such a sin? But then I recognized something that you and I have a hard time recalling about our own lives. I am not perfect either. A man or woman after God's heart is not perfect, but they will deal with their sin, no matter what it is, God's way.

Finally, if you are after the heart of God, you will seek Him. David wanted nothing less than to be back in the walk of faith, with a heart that worshipped and walked in fellowship with his God. So shall it be with each of us.

Lest you read this and decide like so many, "Well, God did not require the throne from David. What could be so bad enjoying a little sin? I am willing to take the risk!" Just remember, David could choose his sin, he could not choose his consequences. There were four to his sin. One, the baby that he and Bathsheba had conceived died. Two, one of his sons murdered his other son. Three, one son raped his daughter; and finally another son ran David out of the kingdom.

Always remember, "Your choices today determine your lifestyle tomorrow!"

Let me ask you, when was the last time you sought God? When was the last time you prayed and just fellowshipped with Him in order to build that love relationship with your heavenly Father? A man or woman after God's own heart will seek the heart of God.

6

ENOCH:
WALKED WITH GOD

*Have you ever thought about the fact
that people last forever -- either in relationship
with God or estranged from His presence?*
Rick Rusaw

*O*f all the men and women in the Bible, Enoch has always been one of my favorites. There is something special about one where God gives this by-line to his life, "Enoch walked with God." That is a tag I would love to have God place on me at the end of my earthly life. Simply put, "Frank walked with God." Doesn't that have a nice sound to it?

When one sets out to discover the secrets to Enoch you will be hard pressed for there is not much written in the Scripture concerning him. The writer of Hebrews writes a little about his legacy.

> *By faith Enoch was taken up so that he should not see death; AND HE WAS NOT FOUND BECAUSE GOD TOOK HIM UP; for he obtained the witness that before his being taken up he was pleasing to God. And without faith it is impossible to please Him, for he who comes to God must believe that He is, and that He is a rewarder of those who seek Him. (Hebrews 11:5-6)*

The Book of Genesis tells us of a man by the name of Jared (Genesis 5:20). He was significant because he was the father of Enoch. Then the scripture records this for us.

> *And Enoch lived sixty-five years, and became*
> *the father of Methuselah. Then Enoch walked with*
> *God three hundred years after he became the father of*
> *Methuselah, and he had other sons and daughters. So*
> *all the days of Enoch were three hundred and sixty-*
> *five years. And Enoch walked with God; and he was*
> *not, for God took him. (Genesis 5:21-24)*

The total years of Enoch here on the earth were 365. These years for Enoch were filled with building such a dynamic relationship with God that God wanted every person who came after Enoch to know that this man discovered the importance of walking with God.

In all fairness, the life of this man is reduced to just five or six verses in the Bible. However short these verses may seem, they reveal several things about the man. It doesn't take long for one to pick up on the theme. Enoch was one that loved God because he knew God. Out of this love relationship and the knowledge he had gained from God, he dedicated his life to walking with Him. So special was the relationship that God and Enoch shared, God evidently decided to demonstrate for us how to do the same.

Robert Baker, in an article called "Country Road 13" in *Christianity Today* made an outstanding statement to which we all can relate. He said… "As I grow older in life I care less about what people think about me and more about what God thinks about me because I expect to be with God much longer in my existence."[1] Now that is something to ponder. The challenge is to live with an eternal perspective.

Enoch

Cruising through the life of Enoch, you will find that he was a man who was concerned about what God had to say about him. For Enoch, it put everything in perspective to think that God is watching his life. He was cognizant of the fact he was building a legacy. God was listening to everything he said and was recording it for all eternity. This should remind each of us that we have a great responsibility.

As I studied the life of Enoch and thought about my three children, there are two things I really want to make sure they have settled in their lives. First, I want them to know they have entered into a personal relationship with God through His son Jesus Christ. I want them to know Christ as Lord and Savior of their life. I do not want them to come to the end of their journey here on earth and only hope they knew Christ as Lord and Savior. I want them to know Him. I want Stephen, Jonathan and Kristen to walk with God daily. I want them to know beyond a shadow of a doubt they were saved and lived the promised abundant life. Remember, it was Jesus himself who gave us such a wonderful promise.

> *The thief comes only to steal, and kill, and destroy; I came that they might have life, and might have it abundantly. (John 10:10)*

Oh, how I desire that for them.

As a pastor, I have stood beside caskets of people's loved ones and heard them lament how they were unsure of their family member's spiritual condition. They will come up next to me and say, "Pastor, I wonder if Dad ever gave his life to Jesus Christ? Pastor, I never knew if Mama ever came to know Jesus. Pastor, what about my brother or sister? Where are they now?" Please understand, at that point it is too late to be worrying about their relationship with Christ. I want to make sure my family has settled that issue of knowing Jesus Christ personally as Lord and Savior.

A dear lady was burdened about her husband who was lost. She knew if he died he would go straight to Hell. She began to pray, "God, just work in his life. Make it so one day he will have a desire to go to church with me and come to know Jesus as his Lord." One Saturday night he walked into their den and just totally blew her away. He announced, "Honey, I don't know why but I'm going to church with you tomorrow." When she went to bed she was excited, ecstatic and full of exuberance as her prayer was about to be answered. Maybe there are some sweet ladies that are reading this who know what this dear wife was feeling. All night long she couldn't sleep but prayed continuously while her husband slept, "Lord, save my husband." She would pray, "Lord, at church tomorrow let there be something in my pastor's sermon that will reach my husband's heart and he will be saved."

The next morning he got up, dressed, and was ready to go for the great adventure of church. The husband walked into church and participated with her. Her heart sank as she picked up the newsletter and saw that the pastor was preaching out of Genesis 5. She thought, "Great! My husband is going to be so bored with all those Old Testament names in Genesis 5." She thought as she scanned down through it, how in the world is this going to be used by God to penetrate his heart so that he'll come to faith in Christ? The pastor preached and at the end as was the custom he gave an invitation. Nothing happened in her husband's life but for the next four weeks he would get up, journey to church and listen to the pastor. Finally, on the fifth Sunday at the invitation he slipped out into the aisle. He walked down and gave his life to Jesus Christ. Tears were streaming down his wife's face as God had answered her prayers.

On the ride home from church she said, "Honey, tell me, when did you come to know that you had a need for Jesus Christ?" Her husband said, "Well, honey, it was the very first Sunday I went and the preacher preached out of Genesis 5." She said "You got under conviction then?" He said, "I read down through those names in the Old Testament, the descendants of Adam and he said after every single one of those men's names there was one phrase that stood out to me." She said, "What was it?" He said, "It kept saying '...and he died.' You read about Seth who lived for so many years and then it says, '...and he died.' Then you read about Enosh and you read, '...and he died.'" Then he said, "For the first time in my life I recognized that one day I was going to die, and I needed a Savior and I gave my life to Jesus Christ." If Genesis 5 teaches us anything, it is simply that every one of us will die unless Jesus comes again. Are you ready?

There is a second thing I really desire for my family. I want each of them to know how to walk with God through a real, intimate relationship with Jesus everyday of their existence here on earth. I want their worship of God to be second nature to them. Something should yearn inside their hearts that screams, "Unless I go to be with God's people and worship Holy God, I am not complete as a person. I am not fulfilled."

Sybil Stanton understood such fulfillment does not

come from the pursuits of this world but of that special relationship with God. She wrote an article in *Leadership Magazine* in which she said, "Your purpose in this life has nothing to do with grandiose goals, lofty achievements.... or universal fame that you may acquire....But it's the quiet confidence that even if you never leave your neighborhood, you know that you have lived fully in your life."[2] For those who are searching for this kind of fulfillment I submit to you it only comes from your walk with your heavenly Father. Fulfillment does not flow from some grandiose idea, goal, lofty achievements or world renowned fame but it flows from living in that splendid walk with God.

FULFILLMENT DOES NOT FLOW FROM SOME GRANDIOSE IDEA, GOAL, LOFTY ACHIEVEMENTS OR WORLD RENOWNED FAME BUT IT FLOWS FROM LIVING IN THAT SPLENDID WALK WITH GOD.

Enoch got it! He developed a meaningful life by his faith walk. It was the real deal to the point that God records for us "... and Enoch walked with God." Through Enoch's life we can learn the essentials of this dynamic relationship.

THE PRIORITY OF FAITH

From this one man's life we can learn about the priority of faith. If we are going to walk in an intimate relationship with Christ it will demand faith. In Hebrews 11:5 one reads, "By faith, Enoch was taken up so that he would not see death and he was not found because God took him up for he attained the witness that before he was being taken up he was pleasing to God." I want you to notice three things about Enoch's faith.

The first one is the *universal problem*. Enoch dealt with

the same problem that we deal with in our lives. The sin problem! A long time ago God created Adam and Eve and placed them in the Garden of Eden. God told them they could eat of any tree but this one tree they were not to eat. At this point they walked in perfect fellowship with God. Then it happened. The tempter entered the picture and tempted them to disobey God. They listened to Satan and indulged in the fruit of the tree God had placed off limits. We call this the fall of mankind. Ever since the days of Adam and Eve, we have wrestled with the sin problem in our own lives. The result of that one action has been broken fellowship and relationship with our Creator. Every man has the need for the broken relationship with God to be restored. We need to have a right relationship with our Creator.

Sin always leaves a void in man's life that can only be filled by the righteousness of God Almighty. Mankind over the years has tried their best but futile ways to fill that God void. They go to church with the regularity of a Pharisee. They work the letter of some religious law in hopes it will satisfy. They strive for the wealth of the world thinking it will bring happiness only to be left empty. They party hardy in an attempt to drink and drown away their sorrows and problems in hopes of finding peace and satisfaction only to discover their sorrows always seem to know how to swim. Maybe you have been there. In fact, you may be there

SIN ALWAYS LEAVES A VOID IN MAN'S LIFE THAT CAN ONLY BE FILLED BY THE RIGHTEOUSNESS OF GOD ALMIGHTY.

right now. The only thing that will bring the peace that you are looking for is the intimate relationship with God through

Jesus Christ.

Enoch like anyone else had to realize that sin had left its mark upon his life leaving him empty. It is a universal problem that everyone to this day must deal with and get it right.

In a small church, a Sunday school teacher taught her class of children the lesson of Adam and Eve and the fall of mankind. To make sure she had taught the lesson well she asked a follow-up question to see if they had grasped the material. She said, "Now class, I want to see if you've been paying attention. Because of Eve's sin she received a punishment. What was her punishment?" Everybody was quiet as they looked around the room. One little bright-eyed girl raised her hand enthusiastically and said, "I know! I know! I know!" The teacher called on her saying, "Okay, what was Eve's punishment for disobeying God?" And the young girl said, "She had to crawl on her belly and eat dirt for the rest of her life." Do you know as I read that I chuckled and said "No, no, no." That was not the punishment for Eve. That was placed on the serpent. God's punishment for both Adam and Eve went much deeper. The punishment was a broken relationship with God that left a vacuum in not only Adam and Eve's life but ours as well. It is a vacuum that can only be filled by God.

MAN IS DESIGNED WITH A GREAT CAPACITY FOR GOD.

Oswald Chambers, one of Christianity's greatest devotional writers, once said, "Man is designed with a great capacity for God."[3] Then he says, "Our sin and our individuality keep us from arriving at God."[4] I want you to think about what he said. Every one is created with a capacity for God. However, due to each of us being born into the sin nature that capacity is best described as a vacuum that can only be filled by holy, righteous God. Chambers says that what keeps us from getting to God is our sin and our individuality, wanting to do life our way.

Adam and Eve had a problem that each of us wrestle with each day. It is wanting to be our own god. Chambers states, "The essence of sin then is the refusal to recognize that you and I are accountable to God." Our sin problem is that we don't feel we are accountable to anyone. I have discovered that when I sin it is because for some reason I just don't think I'm accountable to God. Somehow we have bought into one of Satan's greatest deceptions. He has convinced us we are above the God who created us and we will not have to stand up and take responsibility for how we lived here on earth. Yet the truth is one day I will stand before God, as you will, and give an account of my life. I am accountable to God who is holy, just and righteous.

Oswald Chambers says the problem is the essence of sin. Adam and Eve knew this problem all too well. Being their own god was appealing to them. So they bit the deception of Satan. As they chewed on that fruit, it was deadly to them just as it is to us. The real tragedy is the broken relationship with God that puts death to our fellowship with Him. That is the universal problem.

Recently I purchased a new Bible and journeyed back to the pages of Genesis. I studied fresh and anew the story of the fall of mankind. When I came to Genesis 3, it was like God wanted to show me something that I had often overlooked when reading the story. So often we have the propensity to focus on the fall of man that we give little attention to the result of the fall. In verse 24 of this chapter we find this phrase. "So he drove the man out…" The Lord drove them out of the garden. He removed them from a place of fellowship, protection, and a place of right relationship with God who created them and who gave them purpose. The righteous God that He is could not allow sin to reside in His presence so He drove them out. The horrible result was the broken fellowship with God. That is the universal problem even of our day.

But I don't want you to stop there. I want you to see the *unbridled pursuit*. Enoch was suffering from the same thing everyone prior to him had suffered: the unbridled pursuit. The Bible tells us that man pursued what was right in his own eyes. From the beginning it was there. Eve knew this too well. She looked upon the forbidden fruit, she listened to the tempter when he said, "Has God not said…" At that very moment in time Eve looked at the beauty of the fruit and for whatever reason she was willing to exchange her warmth, her love, her fellowship, her completeness with God. She was willing to trade it all in for the beauty of something she beheld in her eyes. How many times have you done the same thing? How many times have you sat there and hindered your relationship with God because something attractive of this world came along and lured you away from intimacy with Him? To me it is strange that the tempter always lures with the appetites of your life. He tailor makes it for you!

Eve traded peace for turmoil, tranquility for the strife of this life. The world broke out in rebellion. Through the fall of mankind sin makes its grand entrance into the world. As you read through the Book of Genesis, you discover a world with hatred in their hearts toward God. How ironic, they turned their back on the One, the very One, who could bring about peace, fellowship, holiness, as well as fulfillment to their hearts, the very things they desired most. It is so true today as well. People are seeking the very essence of God in their lives but they continue to rebel and pursue the appetites of this world. The citizenship of our world is still pursuing their own desires which always leads down the slippery slope to destruction. In Genesis 5, one can read about our society which seems to mirror the society of that day. This should be a big warning to us.

We have seen man's universal problem followed by his unbridled pursuit, but look at the *unmistakable passion*. In the midst of all that in Genesis 5, one must hear God. In the midst of all this rebellion you can hear God say, "Wait just a minute! Out of all these men who have lived, there is one man in this mass of chaos which stood out and his name is Enoch. I want you to know about Enoch. Enoch had a passion for Me." In a society of selfish pursuits and unrighteousness God, through Enoch's life, highlights how one should have a holy passion for Him.

If God is going to highlight Enoch's life then we should learn everything possible from his life. What do we know about him? In Genesis 5, what is said in verse 21 is powerful.

And Enoch lived sixty-five years, and became the father of Methuselah. (Genesis 5:21)

Think with me about this verse of Scripture and its implications. For 65 years Enoch lived in man's condition, which was the pursuit of his own desires. For all these years, as mankind was in pursuit of wickedness, Enoch was pursuing the world just like everybody else. For the first 65 years of his life he did not walk with God…he stood condemned like you and me because he was a sinner. Then in the very next verse there is a sudden change of direction in his life. It reads…

> *Then Enoch walked with God three hundred*
> *years after he became the father of Methuselah, and*
> *he had other sons and daughters. (Genesis 5:22)*

Here he was in pursuit of the world, and then he suddenly is walking with God. There was a transformation that took place in Enoch's life.

Now wait a minute. Let's stop right here. In one verse he is not walking with God and in the next verse God tells us he had a vibrant relationship with Holy God. In fact, it tells us that for three hundred years he walked with God. What happened? I think the birth of his son became a trigger point for Enoch. I want to ask you, what was your trigger point of coming to faith in God? Every person who has entered into a personal walk with God through Jesus has encountered a trigger point where they recognize they were a sinner and had a need for the Savior. There was something in your life that awakened you to your need to walk with God that produced a willingness to do what needed to be done to enter into a relationship with Him! For those of us on this side of Calvary, we understand that means accepting Jesus Christ as our personal Savior. If you have not invited Christ into your life then you may be taking a walk with something or someone but not God.

Here is what it was for Enoch in the Old Testament. I believe the trigger for him was the birth of his son, Methuselah.

Enoch

Don't forget Enoch was the great-great-great-great-grandson of Adam. Can you imagine that family gathering? I know some of you are thinking right now, "No Pastor, if theirs was anything like mine I don't want to think about it." Well, humor me for a moment. When we look around and see all the dysfunctional families today, we would come to the conclusion that we could have fit right in with Enoch's relatives. If you think your family is messed up, just think about his extended family. They were all wicked and evil! They had been hit big time with the sin stick. They were all living perverted lives that were marked by rebellion. He looked around and saw all the sin, wickedness and debauchery and wondered if there was not a better life.

His family, like yours, probably had someone who told stories about their ancestry. Can't you hear them now? "Remember Adam and Eve? Remember how they were placed in that Garden of divine protection and there was a holy, righteous God who loved them, wanted to have fellowship with them, but then they sinned and now we are the result of all that sin!" I believe every time he heard the story as he looked upon all the sin around, something inside of him said "You know, there is a holy God out there who wants to have fellowship with me. I believe He will care for me if I am willing to walk with Him." Then one day his wife tells him she's pregnant. Nine months fly by and as she is walking around one day she suddenly feels a birth pain. They quickly call Dr. Spock over to deliver the baby. No doubt Enoch paced outside the tent and the still air came alive with the crying of his son, Methuselah. When he walked into their nursery the very first time and held that newborn son there was a trigger point and a moment of decision for Enoch. I believe that Enoch looked at Methuselah, then looked around his society, perverted and sin hardened, then he said something like, "You know what? I don't want my son to experience what I have experienced. I'm going to give my life to Holy God who loves me and desires fellowship with me." He placed his faith in God. The Scripture says in Hebrews 11 "by faith, Enoch…" By faith he gave his life to holy God. By faith! All of a sudden there was a passion that was burning in his life. His passion was to know God with all of his heart. His faith led him to set out to walk with God. The priority of faith is of utmost importance if you desire to walk with God.

THE PRINCIPLES FOR FAVOR

From Enoch we can also learn about the principles for favor. When he placed his faith in God, there was favor that flowed from God toward Enoch's life. I call this the principle for favor.

There are three things I want you to see. First, I want you to see the statements concerning Enoch's walk with God. Hebrews 11:5 speaks of this special relationship.

> *By faith Enoch was taken up so that he would not see death; and he was not found because God took him up; for he obtained the witness that was before his being taken up he was pleasing to God.*

The Scripture declares that he walked with God. Now what does that mean? Matthew Henry Commentaries state that Enoch was really imminently, actively, progressively, preservingly, religious in his conformity to God, in his communion with God. Let me say it in a way that is clearly understandable. Enoch had one drive in his life and that was to know and to walk with God every day of his life. The priority and obsession of his life was God.

Could you imagine what would happen in our world if Christians had the same obsession as Enoch? It is so hard for parents to convince their children that God is everything to them when they relegate Him to just one hour per week. Parents do sound pretty hollow to their children when they say to others they are followers of Christ but can only do so at eleven

IF GOD IS YOUR PRIORITY THEN HE WILL BE EVIDENT IN YOUR LIFE.

o'clock on Sunday morning. What if a husband said to his wife, "I love you with all my heart but I will only see you on Friday nights? Don't call me or drop by to chat, I'll only visit with you on Friday's." I promise you she would not feel too loved and that marriage probably will end up in the tank before too long. If God is your priority, then He will be evident in your life. He will show up in your giving, serving, worshipping, ministering and witnessing. Those who are obsessed with God are just that – obsessed. All hypocrisy will fall away. It is one thing to drive your kids all over the place to meet the many demands as you pursue the world and then before they fall asleep at night you say, "Oh by the way you do know we love God." It is altogether another matter to be genuine in your walk.

TO SAY YOU LOVE HIM AND NEVER HAVE A PASSION FOR WHAT HE IS UP TO IS HYPOCRISY.

A family that loves God will be around the people and the things of God. To say you love Him and never have a passion for what He is up to is hypocrisy. I want you to understand that does not wash with your kids and it definitely does not wash with God! When you say that you want to love God, then you'd better walk with God. You'd better make sure that God is the priority of your life. You need to make sure that God is not getting the leftovers in your life. It's no half-hearted commitment. Everything you do is related to God. Well, the Bible says Enoch had such passion. He walked with God.

The Scripture says he also obtained a witness. Now I want you to understand this is real important that it says he obtained a witness. What does that mean? I am glad you asked. It means that God's Spirit bore witness with his spirit that he was righteous before God because of his faith. Enoch obtained a witness from God.

What does God say about your life? It would be wise to think about it! What will God say about your life on the day you stand before Him? Will He say you are pleasing to Him because you have placed your faith in Him? Now what does it mean to be pleasing? It means that as God saw the evil of mankind He said there was one who would not bend and that was Enoch. Therefore, he was pleasing to God. I wonder as God views the day in which we live and watches our lives, does he see us standing tall or bending to the temptations of this world? Enoch was one who had a conviction about seeking God. What a testimony!

As you strive to understand this man called Enoch, you also encounter steps concerning our walk with God. God says there are three things you need to have in your life. Step one: *you must have life through faith.* Do you know what the Scripture says? For you to claim to be a person of the Kingdom there had to be a moment that you received the gift of eternal life through the One who can give it: Jesus Christ. You must have that personal relationship with Christ. Until then we are dead in our trespasses and sin. The last time I looked, dead corpses don't walk around and for sure they don't talk to others or have fellowship with others. They are dead. There are those who sit in my church and yours on Sunday that are dead in trespasses and sins. That's the reason why some are never moved, never stirred and always watching the clocks. They haven't come to life through faith in Jesus Christ. Some who are reading may be saying, "Boy, he is speaking to me." Friend, you need to make sure you've nailed down your relationship with Christ. Be sure you do it God's way. You need to cry out in repentance and ask Christ into your life.

Step two: *there must be strength through faith*. The only way you can have strength is through exercise. Recently at Collins Hill High School one of our football players went down with a knee injury. One night before one of our games he hobbled up next to me and I asked how he was doing and about his rehabilitation on his knee. He said, "Oh, it's getting stronger every day." I said, "What are you doing?" He said, "I'm exercising it every day." The only way I know to tell you to get strong in your faith with God is every day you exercise that faith no matter what comes. When adversity blows into your life you respond the way God has taught you through Jesus.

You say, "What do I do?" Get into the Word and find Chapter 12 of Hebrews. The writer of Hebrews says we are to lay aside every encumbrance and every sin that easily entangles us. Those are the things which keep us from being pleasing to God. Cast them aside by confessing them to Jesus. Then he encourages us to keep our eyes fixed on Jesus. In verse three it says ...

> *For consider Him who has endured such
> hostility by sinners against Himself, so that you may
> not grow weary and lose heart. (Hebrews 12:3)*

So every day you exercise your faith in Jesus who saved you. He is the author and finisher of our faith. We trust Him to mold us and shape us.

Step three: *there must be conviction through faith.* Listen to the convictions held by Enoch according to Hebrews 11:6.

> *And without faith it is impossible to please
> Him, for he who comes to God must believe that He
> is and that He is a rewarder of those who seek Him.*

Enoch believed firmly that God was real. He also believed that God is the one who rewards those who seek Him. Remember that was his passion. Everyday it must be ours. We should seek Him with all our heart. If we will, He will strengthen and build us up as we exercise our faith in Him.

Finally, we need to see the summons concerning our walk with God. It is the summons to place our faith in the righteous one. Like Enoch there comes a time we must act and pull the trigger. For us, we must place our faith in Jesus Christ. We must come to understand that the Bible says because of his faith in God, Enoch walked with God and he was not for God took him. In a sense, God raptured him.

Do you know that every believer in a sense will not see death? Now some of you will argue the finer points of theology with me at this point and I want to tell you go ahead and argue, but I'm not going to change my mind. One day this body of mine will cease to function and by the world's definition I will die, and they will roll my body down to the front of the auditorium at North Metro. Many will walk by and say, "I thought that preacher said he was not going to die. Look at him, he's dead." No, no, no. I will be as much alive as ever. Even though my body may cease to function and be, the breath of God will still burn within my soul. I will cry out, "Death where is your sting?" Immediately I will begin to breathe in the presence of God. Earthly death for the believer is just the doorway into the everlasting presence of God. It is the door to home.

How does one describe that in our modern day? Let me close the chapter this way. One day a little girl came home from church. Her mother, the consummate teacher, asked the child what she learned from her Sunday school teacher at church. "She taught me about Enoch." The mother said, "What about Enoch? What did she say about Enoch?" "Oh, Mom, she said every morning Enoch would get up and every morning God would come by his house and say, 'Enoch, would you like to take a walk with me? I just want to talk to you.' And Enoch would say, 'Oh, God, I would love to take a walk with you.' One day Enoch got up and God came by Enoch's house and said 'Now Enoch, I really want to walk with you today. I have a lot to say to you.' And Enoch said, 'Oh, God, I really have a lot I need to say to you, too.' So Enoch said, 'Just a minute, God' and Enoch went back in his house and got his coat and even packed himself a lunch and set out on a long journey enjoying a time of fellowship with God. They were just enjoying one another. It was intense, maybe God was saying, 'Enoch, this is what I want out of your life' and maybe

Enoch was saying, 'God, this is what I'm struggling with...'
As they were walking Enoch noticed the sun was beginning
to set. Enoch said, 'Oh, God, it has been a long day. God, I'm
a long way from home. God, we need to turn back. I need to
start heading home.' God looks at Enoch and says, 'Enoch,
you're a lot closer to my home than we are to yours. Why
don't you just come on home with me? And God just took
Enoch on home to God's forever home."

Enoch walked with God! What about you? Can that be
the legacy of your life?

SHADRACH, MESHACH AND ABEDNEGO
THE SEMPER FIDELIS GANG

The more we trust the sovereignty of heaven,
the less we fear the calamities of earth.
Anonymous

*T*he believer is called to make a real difference in the world. It really doesn't matter where you find yourself, if you are planted there that is exactly where God plans for you to have maximum impact. For most it is a pretty safe environment; however, there may be times when you may have to risk it all to stand up for your convictions. We must be willing to always be faithful to our Lord.

Recently one of my nephews, Ricky Wedgeworth, joined the Marines. He is now part of the Few—The Proud—The Marines! I am proud that he is serving our great country. When joining the Marine Corps there is a motto that is drilled into these young people, "Semper Fi." This is a special motto for anyone who has served our country in this branch of our military. It is a Latin phrase which means, "always faithful." Any person who puts on the uniform understands he represents the best and will always be faithful to his country and to his fellow soldiers. Loyalty, faithfulness, and total abandonment is the order for their lives. It does not matter where they are called to serve around the world; their commitment to their country never changes. At times they are met with resistance, yet they are always faithful. They may find themselves in less than desirable situations and circumstances, yet they are always faithful.

When you give your life to Jesus Christ, you have signed up for the most wonderful and exciting life a person could ever experience. We are called to always be faithful in the service to our Master and Lord. As Christians we are to live totally abandoned to Him. It is God's call upon our lives. The high calling from our Master is to be light to the world that is full of darkness. As we set out to be light in this dark and perverse generation, it will make for some interesting times.

Think about what would happen if Christian teenagers really made a commitment to always be faithful to Christ. If one day they rolled out of bed and said, "God, today I'm going to be totally abandoned to You." If every teen would join the "no more excuses club" instead of the "compromise club" could you imagine what would happen on high school campuses across America? Could you imagine if every adult who claims to be a Christian decided to stop playing church on Sunday and said, "Okay, God, You have all of me 24/7"? I guarantee there would be a seismic change in our society. The spiritual awakening that Christians have been praying for would occur. Instead of the church limping along void of power, respect, and impact, it would march in victory and strength. I believe we would see a nation crying out in repentance and a seeking of God as we have never seen in our history.

FOR THERE TO BE A FRESH MOVE OF GOD IN THIS DAY, IT WILL TAKE A MAJOR ADJUSTMENT IN THE FAMILY OF GOD.

For there to be a fresh move of God in this day, it will take a major adjustment in the family of God. We are going to have to make a radical turn in the concept of what it means to be a Christian. We will have to come to the altar daily and crucify our flesh to the cross and be willing to be different from this old world and its influence in our lives. We must be willing and ready. Yes, willing to be strangely odd to this world and ready to suffer abuse, ridicule, mockery, and the venom from those who do not know our heavenly Father in hopes of winning them.

In the New Testament there are times we read a principle, a truth to live by, and if we search carefully we will discover this truth in an Old Testament story. Let me share with you a story from the book of Daniel that demonstrates a truth that is proclaimed in the New Testament book of I Peter. Peter is encouraging Jewish believers to live strong for the Lord in the midst of persecution. Their character and conduct must be above reproach for Jesus. The Christian should never find it strange when faced with fiery trials because of our faith. From the beginning of Christianity this had been true. In fact, as we stand tall and endure the persecution and remain faithful, we will be glad "with exceeding joy" (I Peter 4:12-13).

In Peter's letter he gives a tremendous truth that we need to heed.

> *Beloved, I urge you as aliens and strangers to abstain from fleshly lusts, which wage war against the soul. Keep your behavior excellent among the Gentiles, so that in the things in which they slander you as evildoers, they may because of your good deeds, as they observe them, glorify God in the day of visitation. (I Peter 2:11-12)*

Legacy

The Scripture says "we are to live as aliens." These two verses are power-packed. Let me capture it for you. "Only when you look differently from the world will you be able to demonstrate the difference God has made in your life to the point those in the world will desire God." Something is wrong if those who cruise around your life never desire your Jesus. Yet, when you are totally abandoned and stop compromising with the world, you will see God do a great work.

> **SOMETHING IS WRONG IF THOSE WHO CRUISE AROUND YOUR LIFE NEVER DESIRE YOUR JESUS.**

Some will argue, "Pastor, you don't know the pressure we all live under every day to compromise!" Believe me, I live with the same pressures that you do each day. If you are abandoned to Christ, you will face the heat of the fire. Remember I said you can find a truth in the New Testament, and if you study the Old Testament you will find a story that bears out the truth as it was applied in someone's life? Let me share the story of Hananiah, Mishael and Azariah. (Their names would later be changed to Shadrach, Meshach, and Abednego.) These three men were living with their friend Daniel in captivity. They were "aliens" for sure and yet they would not compromise no matter what pressure was applied. Let's look at the biblical account of three young men who were totally abandoned to God.

THE DEMAND FOR COMPROMISE

Notice the development in the story. According to the Word the mighty king had a dream one night that plagued him. For the sake of his life he could not interpret the dream. It bothered him so much that he invited all the wise men of

118

Babylon in to interpret his dream. The Bible says he called all the magicians, astrologers, sorcerers and the Chaldeans and commanded them to tell him what his dream meant. He even gave them a little incentive. "If you can tell me the dream and what it means," Nebuchadnezzar said, "you will receive gifts from me; however, if you cannot interpret the dream then here is what is ahead for you. I will cut you up piece by piece and your houses will be turned into an ash heap" (Daniel 2:2-5). Talk about motivation! Now that is motivation! I think I would have said, "King, I'm going into the desert for a time of study and will return in 100 years. Long live the king!" I would have run as fast as I could, never to return. Of all these wise men, not a single one of them could do what the king had asked. No, not one! Nada! They were in trouble with a capital "T."

It infuriated the king so he decided to have every one of them put to death (Daniel 2:5,12). He started the massacre and was even looking for the young Hebrew boy by the name of Daniel and all his friends in order to put them to death. Daniel heard about all of this and went to the chief bodyguard, Arioch, and told him he could interpret the dream (Daniel 2:16). He returned to his friends and said, "Pray!" Daniel and his friends knew that only God could see them through this set of circumstances. I hope you have learned that same truth. All things are possible with God! All one has to do is call out to God and He is always there to hear our cry. Everyone who claims to believe should be so close to God.

Thomas DeWitt Talmadge once quipped, "God puts His ear so closely down to your lips that He can hear your faintest whisper. It is not God way off yonder, it is God way down here—up close..."[1] Evidently during this time of exile for these young men, they had learned to pray to God and converse with the One who cared for them. Do you know what they knew about God in prayer? They knew exactly what every person of prayer comes to understand. Robert Murray McCheyne states it best: "God will either give you what you asked or something far better."[2] These boys would demonstrate this later in their experience of walking by faith.

They were in desperate times. Their lives were on the line and if there was ever a time for God to show up and speak up, it was now. They needed God to come through. Abraham Lincoln knew of this desperation. He once wrote, "I have been driven many times to my knees by the overwhelming conviction that I had nowhere else to go. My own wisdom and that of all about me seemed insufficient for the day."[3] All they had to do was look around and see the killing of the wise men to know they were in the big league and needed God.

As these boys retreated to their prayer closet, God heard their plea. They prayed for wisdom, discernment, and especially revelation. God was faithful to answer their prayer and revealed to Daniel the truth of the dream that had plagued King Nebuchadnezzar. They discovered in their moments of prayer that God was faithful.

God was working to a higher purpose than just revealing a dream. God was moving toward revealing in a pagan society that He and He alone was the true God. It would be a "God thing." He allowed these Hebrew boys to be taken into captivity and while miles away from their homeland, He would raise them up to be a witness for Him through their faithfulness. He knew they would be "Semper Fi".

Daniel, with the backbone of a lion, stood before the king and interpreted the dream. This was a moment that defines courage. He held nothing back. When everything was said and done, Daniel and his friends were promoted in this pagan land. They not only were promoted, they prospered.

Faithfulness is the key to prosperity. All one has to do is move around our globe to see this truth born out. I have been privileged to preach in Siberia and Moldova. Both were held under extreme Communist rule. The persecution of the saints in those countries was unbelievable. Today there are great movements of God being experienced because of saints who were faithful when it was tough. At specific times God would grant them favor in unusual ways to further the witness of who God is, even in an atheistic society. God still performs miracles!

Daniel and his friends, Shadrach, Meshach, and Abednego were living in a pagan, perverse, and atheistic country. One must not forget they were in captivity and God performed a tremendous miracle. He reached down in the worst of circumstances and elevated them. God is not limited to boundaries, situations, or circumstances. He is the sovereign God of this universe. You are never out of His reach or presence. He is in control and is always one prayer away. Samuel Chadwick knew the truth that we become conquerors through prayer. He said, "Great supplicants have sought the secret place of the Most High, not that they might escape the world but that they might learn to conquer it."[4]

GOD IS NOT LIMITED TO BOUNDARIES, SITUATIONS, OR CIRCUMSTANCES. HE IS THE SOVEREIGN GOD OF THIS UNIVERSE.

These three boys, Shadrach, Meshach, and Abednego, were about to become conquerors. Remember before these

Hebrew boys were ever captured and deported to Babylon, they had made a commitment to only worship and serve Jehovah God. It was a covenant relationship. Their faithfulness would always invite God's best in their lives. God would always be a Way Maker.

Here is a lesson for each of us. No matter how pagan the environment, God will raise you up if you remain faithful to Him. He will cause favor to rest upon you. From the beginning of their time in Babylon, God did this for these boys. At first it was in their diet. The king was bringing them into the king's service. They were to receive a daily ration of food from the choice food of the king's cupboard (Daniel 1:5). It would be so easy at this point to compromise, but Daniel refused to turn his back on his commitment to God. Just because he was away from all who knew him well, his commitment to God was a conviction of the soul, not a convenience based upon the situation. Daniel purposed in his mind not to defile himself with the king's choice food. In fact, he told the official watching over him of his decision (Daniel 1:8). He told him to test them and see if after ten days their appearance was not better than all the others (Daniel 1:11-12). This was a major test. Would God come through in the pagan culture? Would God raise up these Hebrew boys who were willing to live up to their faith commitment to God? Remember their commitment was inviting God to do His best. The Scripture records it for us...

So the overseer continued to withhold their choice food and the wine they were to drink, and kept giving them vegetables. As for these four youths, God gave them knowledge and intelligence in every branch of literature and wisdom; Daniel even understood all kinds of visions and dreams. Then at the end of the days which the king had specified for presenting them, the commander of the officials presented them before Nebuchadnezzar. The king talked with them, and out of them all not one was found like Daniel, Hananiah, Mishael and Azariah; so they entered the king's personal service. (Daniel 1:16-19)

The test of the food, the interpretation of the king's dream--these boys were making a definite impact in their new environment. God was prospering them (Daniel 2:46-49). Always remember no matter how pagan the environment, God will raise you up if you stay faithful to Him.

THE DEMAND

Now there was a new twist to their situation. The king comes up with a grand idea. He created a golden image the height of which was sixty cubits and its width, six cubits. He set it up in the plain of Dura. He then called all the rulers, officials, and people from all across his kingdom. He gave out a serious decree. When they heard the orchestra playing, everyone was to bow down and worship the golden image. If anyone refused, they would be cast into the fiery furnace. Refusal was instant death (Daniel 3:1-6).

Speaking of peer pressure, here it is live and in color! Could you imagine walking up to the plain of Dura and seeing the great golden image, hearing the decree and turning slowly to see the flames and feel the intense heat, knowing that if you lived up to your commitment to God it was going to be costly? The king was separating the men from the boys. Nebuchadnezzar was not ignorant. He knew whatever people would bend their knees to, they would bow their hearts to. Whatever they would bow their hearts to, they would give their loyalty to. This was a challenge for loyalty.

May I ask a question? Who are you loyal to? Who have you bent your knee toward in your life? For where you bend your knee, you will bow your heart and it will be followed by your loyalty—your life. You need to answer that all-important question, for every day you will face the call for compromise, the call to bend your knee to a false god of this world.

As you contemplate your answer, here is something to strategically place in your mind. Any false god of this world may be just as attractive as the golden image of Nebuchadnezzar, but it will leave you empty and discouraged on the inside. We must wake up and realize our society has a *multiplicity of false gods* bombarding us each day in every way in hopes that we will turn our backs and compromise.

In our society there are false gods of *false prophets*. Americans are so star-struck. If they are on the screen, stage, or in our media, we think whatever they stand for is legit and right. We see Hollywood stars that live together out of the holy bonds of marriage, having children out of wedlock, and cheer them on as though their behavior is right. They promote same-sex marriages and scoff at righteousness, and our culture stands up and applauds. God calls it sin, yet our society accepts their morals and rejects God's standards. The false gods of false prophets.

Also we have what I call the false gods of *physical appetites*. Satan is so shrewd in how he destroys so many in our youth culture. Every person is born with three basic needs. First, the need to be loved; second, the need to be appreciated; and third, the need to be valued as a person of worth. If you are a parent I want you to read carefully at this point. God always expected for these basic needs to be met by the family in the home environment; however, Satan has so many of us preoccupied out in the world that we leave these basic needs to be met in all the wrong places from all the wrong people.

A few years ago a young lady set up an appointment to see me. She had recently been told by her doctor she was pregnant and because she was not married, she had an abortion. She was living with the pain and guilt of the abortion. Her life was devastated. In the course of our time together, the question was raised as to why she had engaged in premarital sex. Her answer was revealing. She said, "I guess I was looking for someone to love and value me." As the old country song declares, "She was looking for love in all the wrong places."

You, my friend, are loved and greatly valued by God so much that He gave His Son, Jesus Christ, to die upon the cross for you. Do not bend your knee to the false god of the physical appetite. God has a special mate for you that within the bonds of marriage will fulfill every need of your life.

Third, our society encounters the false god of *materialism*. The one thing killing our homes and families is this false god of greed. Young couples are charging and charging as they live with the belief they must have in the early stages of their marriage what took their parents thirty years to amass. It is placing them in great bondage and the financial pressures are destroying their relationships and marriages.

WE BUY THINGS WE DON'T WANT WITH MONEY WE DON'T HAVE TO IMPRESS PEOPLE WE DON'T LIKE.

Someone has said, "We buy things we don't want with money we don't have to impress people we don't like." When you bend your knee to greed, it will cost you greatly. It may even cost you your life. One church member who lived in a million-dollar home told me, "Pastor, my wife and daughter have such high demands materialistically it is costing me my health. I work all the time to meet their demands." Then he added, "One day they will find my body in a hotel room having died from a heart attack." How sad! It can be destructive and we must get off the merry-go-round before it destroys. Someone once quipped, "We spend the first half of our lives wasting our health to get wealth; the second half of our lives we spend our wealth to get our health back." Always remember greed can be destructive.

Every day we are faced with false gods. When you bend your knee you will bow your heart and give it your loyalty. You will be loyal to whatever you worship. That was the issue for Shadrach, Meshach, and Abednego. They heard the demand for compromise.

THE DECISION ABOUT COMPROMISE

As you face the demands for compromise you must build upon your convictions. The Hebrew boys dug deep into their convictions and knew they could trust God. When faced with compromise your decision always reveals your devotion.

WHEN FACED WITH COMPROMISE YOUR DECISION ALWAYS REVEALS YOUR DEVOTION.

The king nodded and the music started. Immediately everyone with no convictions fell to their knees and worshipped the golden image (Daniel 3:7). There was no God compass in their lives. One must understand a simple principle: "No conviction means you will fall for anything." If you do not stand for anything, you will fall for everything. Shadrach, Meshach and Abednego had a firm commitment to worship only the true God of Israel. Somewhere back home they had made that decision and nothing would cause them to falter. Every believer must nail down their loyalty and commitment. You must decide the focus of your worship.

The music started and everyone started hitting their knees and worshipping. In the midst of all these pagan worshippers stood Shadrach, Meshach and Abednego, refusing to bow. Their decision had been made a long time before the idol was revealed on the plain of Dura and the furnace was fired up. Maybe it was at a summer camp in Jerusalem that God had revealed Himself to them. No matter when it was, they made a decision. The decision was that God would have the total devotion of their hearts. They were totally abandoned to Him. Nothing would turn them

EVERY LEGACY BUILDER MUST UNDERSTAND THE DEGREE TO WHICH YOU WILL COMPROMISE WILL BE DETERMINED BY THE DEGREE OF YOUR COMMITMENT AND CONVICTION TO ONLY SERVE GOD.

away—no king, no golden image, and for sure, no death chamber. Every legacy builder must understand the degree to which you will compromise will be determined by the degree of your commitment and conviction to only serve God. They had made their decision and it revealed their devotion.

We all face moments when we must stand tall when everyone around us is bowing low. As our allegiance and devotion are revealed, be ready because the devil will rebel. The devil and this world will try to force you to bow down and compromise. In this case the devil used a group called the

Chaldeans.

When they refused to bow and worship, the Chaldeans brought them up on charges. Satan always has his group hanging around. No doubt these Chaldeans were envious or jealous of these "aliens" from Jerusalem coming in and being promoted and prospering in their land. They ran to the king like a bunch of tattletales from the first grade. "Oh king! May you live forever!" What a line to win favor! Once they had his attention they reminded him of his decree. "King, did you not instruct all the people of this assembly to listen for the music? By the way, King, if we may say so, it is one fine orchestra you've assembled. Anyway, when we heard the music, everyone was to bow down and worship. Is that not right, King?" The king said, "Yes, that's right." They quickly said, "King, those Hebrew boys that you have taken a liking to refused to worship the golden image. You said those who refused—into the furnace they would go, so we thought you might like to know there are dissenters in the kingdom." You can almost see the smirk on their faces.

The king had a major dilemma on his hands—what would he do? Let me tell you of his dilemma. The decision these Hebrew boys made revealed their true devotion. King Nebuchadnezzar knew he was not the driving force in their lives, but what was he to do?

The king was enraged. He called out for the Hebrew boys to be brought to him. When they were brought before the king he said, "Is it true that you do not worship my gods or the image I have set up?" It was obvious as to the depth of their convictions. The king was willing to give them a second chance to compromise. He actually thought the threat of death would do the trick. It did not even faze them!

Shadrach, Meshach and Abednego

Every follower of God must always remember a simple point: before the demand for compromise ever comes, you should know how to respond. This decision should be determined before the event, not during. For those who work in corporate America, you must determine now how you will respond when the pressure moments to compromise your Christian ethics come your way. You must know what your convictions are before the pressure is applied.

The boys stood up for their convictions. "King, you can fire up the furnace, for we will not bend our knees to your golden image!" The king shouted with anger, "What god is there who can deliver you out of my hands?" Nebuchadnezzar could not understand because he was the mighty King of Babylon. In his mind they should be trembling in fear. However, they held a conviction that no matter what they were faced with, God would see them through. They could count on Him. Here is their response:

> Shadrach, Meshach and Abednego replied to the king, 'O Nebuchadnezzar, we do not need to give you an answer concerning this matter. If it be so, our God whom we serve is able to deliver us from the furnace of blazing fire; and He will deliver us out of your hand, O king. But even if He does not, let it be known to you, O king, that we are not going to serve your gods or worship the golden image that you have set up'. (Daniel 3:16-18)

It is becoming crystal clear who will always stand in the heat of the battle and let their lives count. It will be those who have strong convictions. It will be those moms and dads who have a big view of God, who believe God can lead them through the fiery furnaces of life. Shadrach, Meshach and Abednego had death-defying convictions. What about you? Each of us will face moments when our convictions will be tested. We will have to make a choice, a decision. Do we really believe in God? Do we really believe He will come through for us?

John Piper writes, "Every moment we live before the face of God and before His face there are no forgotten deeds, no disregarded words, and no inconsequential choices. Each moment is a chance to live utterly to His glory."[5]

All three of these young men made a decision they were going to live for God, and if need be, they would die for God (Daniel 3:17-18). They were at total peace, no anxiety. Billy Graham writes, "Anxiety is the natural result when our hopes are centered in anything short of God and His will for us."[6] Their lives and their hopes were centered on God. They were "Semper Fi" and knew God would be faithful to them as well. He would see them through no matter what they had to face. God will do the same for you. It's all a matter of trust.

THE DIRECTION AFTER CONVICTION

The king was furious. He was so angry he brought his wrath of vengeance upon these boys. He looked at them with uncontrolled hostility. In fact, he was so out of control that the Scripture states, "His facial expression was altered toward Shadrach, Meshach and Abednego" (Daniel 3:19). "Fire up the furnace!" was the command. "Seven times more than it is usually heated. Bring to me my best warriors! Tie those boys up and throw them in! Now let's see what their god can do!" You can almost hear the distain in his voice.

Shadrach, Meshach and Abednego

It didn't take long for Nebuchadnezzar to see the might and the power of the true God of Israel. Events unfolded quickly before the king's eyes. The men who threw them in dropped dead because of the heat. When the king looked into the inferno, he leaped to his feet with astonishment and immediately grabbed some of his officials. Face to face, toe to toe, he asked "Were there not three we threw in?" "Yes, sir!" the reply came. Then Nebuchadnezzar blasted, "Well, I see four men in the fire walking around! Who is that fourth one?" The greatest announcement came from the lips of the pagan king, "The fourth in appearance looks like a son of the gods!" (3:25). Literally, he said, "It looks like a divine being!" Much has been spoken as to the identity of the fourth person in the fire. I believe in the sovereignty of God. He does as He pleases and is always pleased in what He does. God is not limited or constrained by this world especially when those who trust in Him are in need.

> **GOD IS NOT LIMITED OR CONSTRAINED BY THIS WORLD ESPECIALLY WHEN THOSE WHO TRUST IN HIM ARE IN NEED.**

In the discussion of who the fourth person was in that burning fire there has been much speculation. There are some who say it was the Angel Gabriel. Even the Jewish scholars believe it to be an angel. However, I have no problem believing this was the pre-incarnate Christ showing up. From the Christian perspective, we know Christ in the fire has a powerful message for you and me. As we live totally abandoned for Jesus to make a real difference, we will go through the fire at times. No matter how hot the fire society hurls our way, we are not alone. When we are thrown in the fire, Jesus is there to see us through. He always shows up, never early, never late. Jesus is always right on time.

While King Nebuchadnezzar tried to bring his wrath of vengeance, the Lord brought His work of victory. When you stand alone, even in the fire, people will see the glory of the Son of God in and through your life. When the fires of life come your way, that is when your faith must shine the brightest.

Years ago I was in the furnace that was not of my choosing nor enjoyment. However, I would be the first to confess I learned one of the greatest lessons of my life. I learned only those who suffer most have the opportunity to demonstrate great faith. All three demonstrated great faith and God delivered them.

... ONLY THOSE WHO SUFFER MOST HAVE THE OPPORTUNITY TO DEMONSTRATE GREAT FAITH

The king saw it happen before his very eyes and made a significant declaration in the land of Babylon.

> *Nebuchadnezzar responded and said, 'Blessed be the God of Shadrach, Meshach and Abednego, who has sent His angel and delivered His servants who put their trust in Him, violating the king's command, and yielded up their bodies so as not to serve or worship any god except their own God. Therefore, I make a decree that any people, nation or tongue that speaks anything offensive against the God of Shadrach, Meshach and Abednego shall be torn limb from limb and their houses reduced to a rubbish heap, inasmuch as there is no other God who is able to deliver in this way'. (Daniel 3:28-29)*

Shadrach, Meshach and Abednego

Then the postscript of the events states,

> *Then the king caused Shadrach, Meshach and Abednego to prosper in the province of Babylon (Daniel 3:30).*

Remember, you are called to be an alien in this land. You will never fit into this old world. You are called to let your light so shine so God can use you to impact your realm of influence.

THE KEY TO BUILDING A STRONG LEGACY IS FOUND IN TOTAL ABANDONMENT AND FAITHFULNESS TO GOD.

The key to building a strong legacy is found in total abandonment and faithfulness to God. As He puts us out into this world to be salt and light, to be an influence, to make a difference, the one ingredient that will always bring God's victory and prosperity in our lives is that we are always "Semper Fi", always faithful.

Legacy

Modern Day Legacies

See your struggle as God's canvas.
On it He will paint His multicolored Supremacy!

Max Lucado

The only source of Life is the Lord Jesus Christ.

Oswald Chambers

BLESSED BROKENNESS
THE LIFE OF KIMBERLY HOBGOOD

*Only those who suffer most have the
opportunity to demonstrate great faith!*
Frank Cox

*T*he pretty little blonde was as cute as a china doll.
She was not that tall and at a quick glance, one realized
something was different about her, strangely different.

She walked up with a crippled strut and said, "Hi,
I'm Kimberly Vaughn." It didn't take long to recognize she
had a bubbly personality. In fact, over time one discovered
Kimberly was a great deal of fun to be around. God blessed
her with a character that had been
refined by brokenness in her life.

> ... YOU ARE EITHER IN A STORM, HAVE JUST COME OUT OF A STORM, OR YOU'RE HEADING TOWARD A STORM.

When people go through tragedy
it challenges them to examine every
value they hold sacred within. For
most, the storms or struggles come later
in life. One who lives for any period of
time knows that life can be a series of storms. I tell people you
are either in a storm, have just come out of a storm, or you're
heading toward a storm. There is no such thing as living a
storm-free life. It is through these experiences that God sifts
all your belief systems to develop within you the character
and holiness of God. We call it "being refined by fire."

For this bubbly little blonde named Kimberly Vaughn,
she came into this world in the midst of the refiner's fire. At

every birth we check to make sure all the toes and fingers are in place. We feel it represents "normal." We all want our babies to be normal. No doubt this was the prayer of Norman and Linda Hamilton Vaughn of Kingsport, Tennessee yet within hours of her birth, they would discover their baby girl was anything but normal. In fact, it would take years before her life reflected anything of normalcy. She was physically broken.

In America we throw away or discard that which is broken. A toy breaks—out to the trash can it goes. A car is wrecked and we total it out because it will never be the same again. But what do you do when it is a broken child? Well, you love, caress, cry and do what you must do to discover God's blessings even through brokenness. This is exactly what Kimberly has done throughout her life, finding God's blessings through the pain of her brokenness.

For Kimberly it all began on March 19, 1968, in Kingsport, Tennessee. Celebration was in the air as the Vaughn family welcomed their daughter into the world. The excitement was genuine because this was their first baby and on top of everything, it was a girl! Kimberly's mom, like most ladies, always dreamed of a beautiful little girl she could dress up and play with like a cute little doll. The time had arrived and after 72 hours of grueling labor the long anticipated celebration kicked off with the announcement, "It's a girl!"

Her dad was a typical dad—smitten. The first time he saw his daughter she was wrapped in a little pink blanket with her nose poking through, the face of an angel, sweet and innocent. The innocence of that great celebration would be short lived. The joy subsided as the doctors approached the family with some disturbing news. "Mr. Vaughn, we have found a mass at the base of your daughter's spine. She has Spina Bifida."

With this tragic news, their lives began to change. This was not a normal birth, normal child, normal anything. Her mom and dad were young and were stunned by the news and even more with all the implications of what lay ahead for them and their firstborn. The questions began to flow. "Will she ever walk? Will she ever do anything that normal kids love to do?" The storm was gathering in the Vaughns' lives. Their lives would be anything but normal from that day forth.

For believers, storms drive us deeper into our faith or they should. As the family hit the depths of their circumstances, they felt the arms of their everlasting Father wrap around them as a couple. They felt their heavenly Father do what He does best. He loved them and showed He cared. God reminded them that He was the sovereign God and this had not caught Him by surprise. He was in control and it would be alright. What a promise in the face of darkness and uncertainty!

FOR BELIEVERS, STORMS DRIVE US DEEPER INTO OUR FAITH...

The journey would be a long one. At four months Kimberly's parents drove to the Shriners Hospital in Greenville, South Carolina. The journey would demand great faith and it would cost a great deal of money, which the Vaughn family did not have a lot of at the time. However, God is so good as He makes provisions for our every need. The provision of God flowed to the Vaughns through the Shriners Hospital. This benevolent ministry would be the way God would provide for Kimberly's physical needs.

The doctors examined Kimberly and then made the diagnosis that would involve a series of operations to help correct her feet, legs, hips, and back. There was a ray of hope and doctors wanted to begin right away. "Right away"; as those words filtered through Kimberly's parents' minds, they were having to adjust that today was the day her journey to healing would begin. As in most cases where severe action must be taken, it can be overwhelming as it was for Kimberly's parents. "Right away" in this situation was that very day.

With mixed emotions, as any parent could imagine, they handed their four-month-old daughter over to a group of strangers. With a kiss goodbye, her parents got back in their car and drove the five hours back home, hearts breaking, tears flowing, yet resting in the arms of their everlasting Father that would give them strength.

Henry Blackaby says, "When you face a crisis of belief, what you do next reveals what you really believe about God."[1] On this day the parents demonstrated a great deal of what they believed about God. Many times they had read from the Word of God about His strength, provision, and care for every need in their lives. Now it was time to put action to their faith. Over time Kimberly would learn to trust God in a dynamic way just as her parents were demonstrating on this very day.

WE HAVE TO GO THROUGH MANY EXPERIENCES IN ORDER TO GET THE SPIRITUAL VISION WHICH IS NEEDED TO SEE THE DIVINE PLAN. A FILM IS DEVELOPED IN A DARK ROOM.

Faith was going to be developed in these young parents. Someone anonymously wrote: "We have to go through many experiences in order to get the spiritual vision which is needed to see the Divine plan. A film is developed in a dark room."[2] The Vaughn's were definitely in a dark room and only God could develop their faith.

Linda's mind, I'm sure, drifted to the thoughts of what they were faced with so early in life. Most parents were getting up for midnight feedings or to change a diaper. Looking out the window on the long drive home, the thought of just changing a diaper was far more welcoming than the reality. The prayer uttered would be simple but would carry great significance as God continued to teach them to trust Him. "Everlasting Father, watch over my baby. Heal her and make her whole." She turned to the only One she could, God the Father.

The journey of faith is lengthy so it seems to the one required to travel on it; however, in comparison to eternity it is just a short journey. For the next ten years, the Vaughn family grew very familiar with the trip to Greenville. It was their life: Greenville, surgery, recovery, home. It ran in cycles. It was a scenario which was repeated often, all under the compassionate care of their everlasting Father.

As Kimberly was growing up the hospital was becoming a second home. It would carry hours of loneliness and at times despair. There was a ritual she and others grew accustomed to. They lived for the weekends. A lady would announce over the loudspeaker, "Parents, you may now go visit your children." The children would sit, if they were able, at the end of that long hallway and watch with great anticipation as to whose parents would be coming. Kimberly's heart would flutter when she saw her parents come around the corner. She cherished those visits as any young child would, especially when her brothers would accompany her parents.

As much as Kimberly loved her brothers, they were ever concerned about their sister. Unable to go directly to their sister, they would stand outside a large glass window and they would all blow kisses to one another. The brothers, knowing what their sister was going through, just wanted to bring some joy into her life. They spared no expense. One time they brought a frog in a jar. They poked and jolted the frog causing it to jump around, entertaining Kimberly with a one-frog circus.

It did not take long for Kimberly to realize she was different. When her brothers left for school, she would leave and go to a special center if she was able. When her brothers spoke of their experiences, she would dream of being normal and attending real school. She cherished the idea of going to class, special science projects, and yes, even the homework. Brokenness of the body could, in a weaker person, create a brokenness of heart and spirit. This would not be the case with Kimberly. Instead, God created in her a drive to be with other children and even to teach.

God, the Everlasting Father, would not only bring healing to a broken body but also give the desires of the young heart. He supplied the energy, strength, and ability for her to go to high school and even on to college. She would graduate with the vision of teaching children in public school. Her parents encouraged her to stay near her hometown, as any parent would with a desire to watch over her. Yet Kimberly knew the best thing for her was to strike out on her own. For the love of His special child, He provided Kimberly with her first teaching job in Gwinnett County, Georgia.

This was a big deal! Secretly her first dream of overcoming her physical brokenness was being realized. Her first day of teaching could be classified as one of the most exciting days of her life to that point. The morning went by uneventfully but there was a special moment that had finally

Blessed Brokenness

arrived. She was taking her fourth grade class to lunch. They were pros at the routines of the school cafeteria. The students had been jumping through the hoops for three years. For Kimberly, this was her first day ever to eat in a school cafeteria. She was overjoyed! It was a day of enormous magnitude. The meal was cheese pizza, how appropriate! The little girl, because of her physical condition at one time, who could not go to school, was now indoctrinated into the joys of teaching in an elementary school. She was elated!

Kimberly has thrived as a teacher. Twelve years later she was elected by her faculty as the Teacher of the Year at Rock Springs Elementary School. No master's and no doctorate, but a whole lot of passion and love for her students, a love which was instilled within her by her everlasting Father.

Remember the question her parents asked? "Will our daughter ever walk?" Not only was she walking, she was working and making a great contribution to life. Over the years the question had to flow through Kimberly's mind, "Is there someone out there to see beyond my brokenness and see the blessing within bestowed by my heavenly Father?" Kimberly had a secret desire of the heart. Like anyone else, she desired a companion, a completer to her life, a husband to love her for who she was.

In Georgia, God had not only a special job for Kimberly, He also had prepared a young man named Chris Hobgood. Chris was tailor-made for Kimberly, a sincere follower of Christ in whom God had done a work of spiritual sensitivity that few ever achieve. In fact, Chris never saw the brokenness, just the blessing. She was, and would prove to be, the greatest gift and blessing to Chris. It is definitely a marriage made in Heaven.

Legacy

The blessings for Chris would be the many lessons she would share. Remember God had been teaching her from birth through her brokenness. She had a focus that would not allow her to feel sorry for her body, which may not be as strong as others, but her determination more than made up for it. Just the blessing of "she can do all things through Christ who strengthens her" would be a great encouragement to anybody and especially to the special man God had prepared for her. She never complains because over the years God has proven Himself faithful to little Kimberly Vaughn. He has sustained her every need and given her the desires of her heart.

Theirs is a glorious love story. Kimberly and Chris met at North Metro First Baptist Church. It was at a fellowship they spent a few minutes talking with one another and Kimberly poured Chris a soda. He must have made a good impression because Kimberly called him up and asked him out for a non-date. Chris said yes and they had a great first non-date. It was so great that Chris knew she was the one and 59 days later he popped the big "M" question. "Kimberly, will you marry me?" With the pause of the moment, she knew her heavenly Father had been faithful to her again. She instantly said, "Yes!" and God continued to pour out His blessings upon little Kimberly Vaughn.

The legacy of her story does not end with Prince Charming there is so much more. What more could happen to little Kimberly Vaughn, whose life seemed to be destined for despair with not much hope of joy and fulfillment? Well, the blessings continued to flow. God never does anything halfway.

After a couple of years of marriage, God called Chris and Kimberly into the ministry. They moved to North Carolina to attend Southeastern Baptist Theological Seminary. It would be here God would continue His mighty work in Kimberly's life. As with most seminary wives, she worked to help put Chris through school by teaching kindergarten at a nearby elementary school. Teaching children was a joy for Kimberly. She fostered a secret desire of being a mother. She wanted to have a child of her own to hold and love. Her heart was crushed along with Chris after her latest medical exam. The doctor shared with her that due to the impact of Spina Bifida on her body, she would never have children. She always wanted to be someone's mom. She and Chris sat on their sofa and cried together, having heard the shattering news. The pain was almost unbearable. God spoke to her heart and said, "Kimberly, look at your life. I have been so faithful to you and I will be faithful to you again, but you will have to trust Me."

Trusting God is easier said than done many times, even for the most faithful. As school started, Kimberly would encounter little Marlee Mountcastle. Marlee was every teacher's dream and Kimberly took to her instantly. One day they were sitting on the playground together and Marlee asked a painful question in a way only an innocent preschool child could. "Mrs. Hobgood, why don't you have any kids at your house?" Kimberly's heart was breaking on the inside because she wanted to be a mom. "Well, Marlee, God hasn't given me any yet." Marlee looked back and with great confidence announced, "I'm going to tell Him to give you some!"

A voice of an innocent preschooler or was it the voice of God through Marlee Mountcastle? At a parent conference Marlee's mom asked, "Mrs. Hobgood, have you been talking with the class about wanting to have a baby?" Surprised by the question, Kimberly said, "No, that could get me fired. Why do you ask?" "Every night Marlee prays the same prayer…

> *Dear God, please make Mrs. Hobgood a*
> *mommy. She would be so good at it and Lord, please*
> *let it be a little girl that's cute like me. Amen.*

What a prayer! Kimberly never shared with Marlee's mom what the doctor shared with her. Later she received a card with a present from Marlee and her mom. The card said, "Dear Mrs. Hobgood, we're still praying for your miracle!"

God is in the miracle business. Time went on. A couple of years went by and one morning Kimberly started feeling sick. After a few days Chris convinced her to go to the doctor. To everyone's amazement the doctor announced she was eight weeks pregnant! Thirty-one weeks later Kimberly gave birth to Marlee Grace Hobgood, perfect and healthy. God has so completed Kimberly Vaughn Hobgood. Through her brokenness God has so blessed her. To God be the glory!

Kimberly is a tremendous testimony to the faithfulness of God. Her greatest praise to God is found in the Book of Psalms 139:14-15,

> *I will give thanks to You, for I am fearfully*
> *and wonderfully made; wonderful are Your works,*
> *and my soul knows it very well. My frame was not*
> *hidden from You, when I was made in secret, and*
> *skillfully wrought in the depths of the earth.*

When her physical brokenness could have destroyed her, Kimberly had great faith in her heavenly Father. He would make her whole and be faithful in fulfilling each of her

Blessed Brokenness

dreams. Every week she reminds those who know her best that she has been blessed by her everlasting Father.

No matter what your circumstances may be, no matter what your journey, the lesson of Kimberly Hobgood's life is a simple but profound one. God is faithful! What a legacy!

Legacy

WHEN FALSE GODS GIVE NO ANSWERS
THE LIFE OF ALAN FAHRING

We grow and mature spiritually through adversity,
not when everything is going smoothly...
in a time of adversity or trouble,
the Christian has the opportunity to know
God in a special and personal way.
C. Everett Koop, former U. S. Surgeon General

W hat does one do when the power of their god is taken away? At best that is exactly what happened to Coach Alan Fahring. At the pinnacle of his career, he discovered that life as he knew it doesn't last forever, at least not here. With a routine visit to his doctor his life would be changed forever. The god that he had served for nearly 37 years could do nothing to lighten his load or at least take away the blow of a doctor bearing the news. . . "Alan, you have cancer."

In America, every boy dreams of playing ball. The culture of the 1950's was much simpler and less complicated than our present day. In fact, looking back on that era in our history can carry a great amount of nostalgia. It was a time when a boy from a small, midwestern town of Salina, Kansas could lay in bed at night and dream of his heroes. He could play every scenario out in his mind. The score would be tied in the bottom of the ninth, the World Series on the line, the count being three balls and two strikes, the next pitch would be historic as well as what the batter would do. Boys across America would dream, yes, pray to have the opportunity to hit the home run like their hero, Mickey Mantle or Ted Williams.

Legacy

That was who we were in Americana and who Alan Fahring was in an age when athletics were pure and innocent.

Born on August 5, 1947, to Lois and Philo Fahring, his journey of life found its genesis. As with most parents, his mom and dad would pour their love and nurture into their son to be sure he had the right values to pursue his dreams in life. His early life would be one that home movies could be made and recorded on the old black and white 8mm -- the family at the lake, Alan skiing behind the family boat, Alan riding his bike down the streets of the small Kansas town he called home.

Investing in their children's lives was the norm in that era. From his early memories, he would recall the pre-dawn hunting trips with his dad on Saturday mornings to hunt quail or pheasant. A dad and his son—male bonding and enjoying life together, a father having an impact on his son.

Philo, his father, was a hard worker who built a business working long hours to provide the American life for his family. The work ethic Alan saw in his dad would provide the stimulus to create the mindset in him to succeed in whatever he chose to do in his life. Whatever young Alan gave his energies to would have his whole commitment because that was what was modeled by his father to him.

The smell of the athletic field was quickly captured in his young mind partly because both his parents were either an athlete or came from families that loved sports. The passion for competition was birthed. Alan's love for sports not only came from his father but also his mother. Lois would put on a glove and spend an afternoon pitching the ball with young Alan to help him fine tune his skills as a baseball player. He was off and running ultimately to discover his natural, God-given ability as a competitor in athletics.

On slow days he would find himself in the family's basement rummaging through the memories of a time gone past for his parents. He would discover that birthed within every child is a desire to know what their parents were like when they were young. He had heard the stories but nothing brought it to life for him like diligently studying through the yearbooks of Salina High School. There they were all lined up, his hall of fame, his dad, Philo, and his two uncles, Mark and Sandy. All three had evidently proven themselves as leaders on the football field, for all three were captains. They were the ones the team of Salina High School looked up to for fifteen years as examples of excellence on the football field.

Any son would be proud and Alan was no different. He would stare at the pictures, then go into the closet and pull out his dad's letter sweater and hold it tight. Little did he know that the seed of being an athlete was growing within.

Everyone has a defining moment when they know they have just made a major discovery that would shape their life. For Alan it was early on that his parents took him to his first Salina High School football game. It was impressive! They were playing Topeka High. The electricity was in the air. People from all over had come to cheer their team to victory. Alan was like a kid in a candy store. The yearbook pictures, the letter sweater, all the stories he had heard were coming alive before his eyes. The sights and the sounds were definitely impressionable. To this day a vivid picture of the stadium fills his mind with every detail crystal clear, even down to his seat. He was seated on the edge where the players would enter the field and he was taking in all the sights and feeling the vibrancy of the crowd. There came a magical moment when he heard the clicking of cleats on concrete and he looked below to see the players preparing to run onto the field. He was mesmerized as the Salina High Mustangs with their clean maroon uniforms charged the field to the roar of the crowd and the impressionable Fahring knew this was for him. He was in his element!

Over time one hopes he can continue a tradition. For a young boy like Alan Fahring, he believed tradition and history were important. No doubt this was instilled by his mom. Salina, Kansas cherished their history when it came to sports. As a kid, Alan was taken by his mom to the local museum in town. Strategically placed was a picture that always captured his attention, and like a seed it planted a heart's desire to live up to the heritage that was his. The picture depicted images of some young men who had walked up from Wards, Kansas and settled the city of Salina. One of these men was his uncle. As one of the founding fathers of his hometown, Alan and his relatives grew up with an understanding it was important to take pride in all that one has done. To him in a sense he was living out the life of a pioneer and that he was to make a mark with the heritage he had inherited. He just sensed a strong lure to be a conquering spirit.

There were many significant people who assisted in shaping the dreams of his life. One was his father, Philo. His dad had a dream as a young man to be a teacher and a coach. As World War II was raging, his dad along with his brothers went to enlist. It was discovered that his father had a heart murmur. He returned and spent a year at Kansas State before running out of money and returned home to eventually become a successful businessman. He had always been Alan's hero and the dream of teacher and coach germinated in the son's heart.

The dream continued to grow through his Uncle Mark. Returning from World War II, the government paid for his college and he became a teacher and coach. As Alan was growing up, every year he received a jersey from the team his uncle coached. He wore the jerseys with pride and dreamed of playing the game.

In his early days he lived within two blocks of the elementary school he attended. In Salina everyone walked to school. Alan and his friends would walk passed what seemed to be an endless playground. America was much simpler in those days and especially in the midwest. It was a time when the bell would ring and all the boys would rush to the playground to spend the afternoon playing whatever the season would call for in sports. Baseball and football were the sports that excited them. The playground was huge in the child's eye of the vacant lot where the heat of competition took place.

In those early days, Alan knew he had the heart of a lion. By every definition of the word, he was a competitor and a winner. His dad would position himself and watch his young son conquer the field. In his son he saw a fierce combatant and would frequently call him over to warn him not to be so rough on the other kids. Rough? Alan could not believe he was being rough as his father described. Philo may have thought his son rough but Alan's philosophy of healthy competition that would guide his life was taking shape.

Alan's approach was not complicated. In fact it was quite simple. "If I'm going to participate, then I was going to give it my all. I was going to do it as hard as I could for as long as I could." There would be a gleam in his eyes as he lined up on the line of scrimmage to play. The heart of the lion roared, "This is my game, my field. They will have to carry me off the field. I am never going to quit! I'm here to win!"

With Philo being a driven successful businessman, to watch his son manifest such a winning attitude had to produce a positive pride in his heart. He was viewing the drive, a personality taking shape that would serve his son throughout his life and even in the battle for his life.

His high school career was stellar. For three years he was a great contributor to the football program at Salina High School. They were a fierce team to deal with to say the least. When their opponents and their fans entered their stadium, they knew it was going to be the battle of a lifetime. Everyone knew they were the powerhouse to beat. Alan only played in one losing game his two years on the varsity.

It was during his high school years that the spiritual foundation of his life was beginning to take shape. As a young child he was dragged to church by his mom and dad. If it was Sunday they were at church, yet there was something alive within him that was vying for his time and commitment. Football was quickly becoming the passion of his life.

While that is true, God was at work through his coach. Kaye Pierce was a man's man and a great football coach. He knew that every boy on his team needed what only Christ could provide. The coach went to an individual who had played in the past and together they started the Fellowship of Christian Athletes chapter at their school. The coach understood the power of his influence and let it be known a person's relationship with Christ was important. When they met for their first meeting, over a hundred boys were there. In the summer, FCA camp was a must. It was there that Alan

When False Gods Give No Answers

first made a decision for Christ, a decision that would come to mean everything later in life.

He wanted to be like his coach—what a life! Every day you get up and get to coach football. He set out on the journey to become a football coach and fulfill his dream. He played college ball under Coach Gene Bissell at Kansas Wesleyan, here again a godly coach who never jammed religion down the throats of his players but modeled Christ to his boys.

The four years at Kansas Wesleyan were outstanding years for the powerhouse competitor that Alan had matured into. He found his place in the game of football. His college career was so tremendous that he was voted twice by the Associate Press Sportswriters to the status of Little All American for small colleges, an honor that few ever attain.

The influence of Gene Bissell was tremendous upon Alan. With a decision already made to go into coaching after his playing days at Kansas Wesleyan, he went to graduate school at the University of Kansas and was a graduate assistant at the small Otto University. It was the building of a coach that would ultimately be used to be a mentor and major influence in the lives of young men.

Alan landed a job at Kansas State University because of his drive. He thought that to be the best one must go to the college ranks to coach. He lasted for one year as an assistant coach at the college level. The questionable ethics of this particular program at the time really caused Alan to look deep within and to ask himself about his values as a coach, but more important, what was the most important thing to him as a man. It did not take long for the real man to stand up.

In every man's life he will come to a moment of

decision. Depending upon his decision will drive the destiny of his life.

Fahring knew his conscience would not allow him to stay in college ball. Not all programs were like what he was experiencing, yet he knew where his heart was leading. He longed for the purity and the innocence of high school football, a place where he could train and mentor young men, a place and position where he could make a difference. Coach Fahring's years, with the exception of the two years he coached at Kansas Wesleyan with his mentor Gene Bissell, have all been spent on the high school field.

Alan became one of the most successful coaches on the high school scene. Always a contender, he built programs in schools who never had a winning tradition and molded them into winners, competitors, and contenders. He had everything going for him, yet in his prime it all came to a startling end. It didn't take place on the high school gridiron but in the sterile environment of his doctor's office.

In July of 1996 Alan and his wife, Dianne, were flying high. He was in the premier job any coach could desire. He was the first head coach at the affluent new school, Collins Hill High School, in Gwinnett County, Georgia. Football in Gwinnett County is king. To be the first coach at what would become the largest high school in Georgia would be any coach's dream. To build a program out of nothing had Alan and Dianne at their zenith.

What was to be the most productive time in Alan's career had suddenly sent him into a storm, not just any storm, but the greatest storm and challenge of his life. The doctor informed Alan that he had cancer! The big "C" word seldom brings any hope to the person it is hurled toward. He was stunned and scared at the same time. The truth is his cancer did not know who it had chosen to go up against. Just by fortitude alone, Alan had always held the title of winner. In his mind, this would be no different. All he needed was for the doctor to prescribe the course of action and his conquering spirit would take over. The heart of the lion would roar and the cancer, like so many of his previous challengers, would retreat quickly from his life.

Surgery would be the answer. He and Dianne were ready. If this is what it would take, so be it. Bring it on! On the day of the surgery there would be a voice familiar to Alan that would call out to him. Alan knew the voice. It was faint at first but recognizable from an FCA camp where he first met this friend. It was the voice of the One who promised never to leave Alan and never to forsake him. In all honesty it had been a while since Alan and his friend had spent time just talking, however the circumstances of life had drawn them together once again. This time their friendship would grow much deeper.

As he laid on the gurney making his way into surgery, Alan realized the god he had served for 37 years had no answers when it came to life and death. It was his true friend, Jesus Christ, who held any hope. Alan called out to his friend whom he had invited into his life as a young athlete. While it had been years, Alan found the presence of Jesus real to him. Through this experience Christ headed Alan on a journey of faith, trust, and heavenly hope that would teach him that even in the storms of life the true conqueror, Jesus, would see him through.

It was about this time in Alan's life that I was invited to be chaplain of Collins Hill High School football team. My son, Stephen, was playing for the coach. One has to believe in Divine Providence. It was not by chance he asked me to serve—no, I believe it was his friend, Jesus, guiding to bring us into a closer relationship. For me, I had lost my first wife to cancer when she was 27 years old. These kinds of struggles teach life lessons that only these trying times can. They were lessons God would use through me to help Alan, yet there would be lessons God would teach me as I have walked with Alan through his journey with cancer.

Our friendship intensified one day a few years after his surgery. Alan is a very private person. He had only spoken with me once directly about his cancer. We were eating at Longhorn's, a local restaurant, and it was brought up as we talked about his relationship with Jesus. Our bonding was taking shape for the intensity of the journey. Alan was open but guarded. Slowly but surely I was moving into the role of his pastor and even better, his friend.

Early one morning my phone rang and a man named Ben Israel was calling from Arkansas. "Frank, you don't know me but I'm calling concerning a mutual friend of ours who doesn't know I'm calling, but he just found out last week his cancer is back. He is devastated. Both he and Dianne are broken. I asked Alan if there was anyone he would trust to talk with about his situation and he mentioned you. He trusts you and I'd like to ask if you would reach out to Alan." I assured Ben I would and immediately called the school. Alan, still the private man, in the course of the conversation asked to come see me. In the afternoon he arrived for this time of moving along the journey of discovering more about his great God.

As he came into my office, I knew it was hard. Remember, he prides himself on being a man's man who up to

158

this experience had always been able to find a way to win. The opponent this time was bigger than the coach. No X's and O's could come up with a game plan. He was staring at eternity in eighteen months. He, like so many others when faced with such prospects, discovered it to be sobering.

As he sat down in my study the tears began to flow. Brokenness did not come easy to this one who always seemed to be in control. I could tell he did not like the fact that I was seeing the tender side of a man who made his livelihood being tough. Remember, this was the biggest storm of his life, a storm that would teach him valuable lessons he could never learn apart from the storm.

Alan and I have enjoyed numerous conversations over the years since that day in my office, many conversations that will stay between close friends and should be left in the privacy of my study. We have a close relationship that would cause me never to infringe on conversations of a man dealing with a unique journey; however, I will share what I have observed from his journey, lessons he has taught me as he has reluctantly entered his own personal storm.

Let's talk about storms for a moment. As I finish this chapter on my dear friend, I am sitting on a balcony in the Caribbean. It is July and we are in the midst of the hurricane season. During a recent hurricane season we saw the devastation of Hurricane Katrina. It literally destroyed New Orleans, a place Dianne and Alan loved to visit. Alan is one of many who has discovered that some of the greatest storms in life do not come by way of raging winds, surging water, or levees collapsing. Instead storms can come through adversity. In Alan's case, it was the storm of cancer. The scenario is familiar in all our lives. One day the sun is shining and life is good. You go to sleep on top of your world, only to get up the next day to be greeted by dark clouds filled with lightning and thunder. For Alan, his storm happens to be cancer. For you it may be divorce, career loss, or sudden death of a loved one. We will all face storms, so we need to learn maybe even through Coach Fahring's personal storm, how to react in the midst of the storm. He has taught me two things concerning storms that I believe will be his legacy.

First, he has taught me facts concerning the storms of life. It doesn't matter what your storm, there are three facts to always remember.

Fact One: Storms come to everyone. Just because you are a preacher or even a head football coach of the largest high school in the state, the gale winds blow in all our lives. Alan asked all the normal questions when it happened to him, "Why is this happening to me?" The answer is found in God's Word. Jesus makes it plain in Matthew 5:45,

> **STORMS COME TO EVERYONE.**

> ...*in order that you may be sons of your Father who is in heaven; for He causes His sun to rise on the evil and the good, and sends rain on the righteous and the unrighteous.*

It rains on everyone. Those who live for God will face storms and even those who live with no thought of God will face storms. We live in a fallen world. Storms can happen to everyone.

Alan was a good man in a noble profession helping to form young men's lives. If anyone should be exempt from storms it would be him. However, the fact of life is simple: if you live long enough you will face a storm.

Fact Two: Storms don't last forever. When you are going through the storm you have a tendency to say, "It hurts so bad!" In the midst of that dark storm you believe you will

STORMS DON'T LAST FOREVER.

never return to normalcy like you knew before. Think about it just for a moment. It would be tragic for you to go through such a struggle and not grow through your experience. Alan reminds each of us that attitude is everything in the storm. No longer does he ask "Why?" but "What? God, what do You want to teach me?" I have watched him move from a very weak walk with God to one that is vibrant and growing. He has realized that learning to live with cancer is the new normalcy of his life. Storms can only control your life based upon your attitude. Alan chose not to allow the storm to control him but has allowed God to show him how to live with it in order to bring glory to God.

Fact Three: Sometimes God may even seem to be silent at the most intense time of the storm. At the moment you think God is silent and has turned his back on you, it will be the very time He will be working for your best.

SOMETIMES GOD MAY EVEN SEEM TO BE SILENT AT THE MOST INTENSE TIME OF THE STORM.

The disciples and Jesus set out on a journey to the other side of the Sea of Galilee. If you have been to that part of the world, you can remember the terrain surrounding the Sea. High hills surround this beautiful area that we romanticize about in the Scripture when it speaks of the Sea of Galilee. The hillsides are full of crevices. There are times

161

when the wind will make its way through those crevices and when the warm air meets the cool water, storms of hurricane magnitude can erupt. It happened to these disciples that day and they did what so many of us do when we're faced with our storms. They panicked. These disciples searched for Jesus only to discover He was asleep on a cushion. (Mark 4:38) "Jesus!" they cried, "Are you not concerned we are perishing here?" Jesus stood up and said, "Hush, be still!" The storm died away instantly. Don't miss this. Storms never silence our Lord nor cause Him to panic. Jesus is always in control. That day on that gurney, Alan discovered Jesus was still there with him and for him. Alan's faith began to grow. The god of football had no answers, but the God of the universe stood up in Alan's life and continues to this day to answer every need in his life. So when you find yourself in the midst of a storm, believe me, God is real. God is there, and He is definitely at work to bring about the good in your life. It is a journey of faith.

Secondly, Alan has taught me faith commitment in the storms of life. The faith journey has been tremendous in the coach's life. He is part of an E-Group (encouragement group) in our church. Nine men have come together to be an encouragement to one another in our journeys. We have been meeting for several years, and I have watched his faith grow by leaps and bounds. God has taught us through Alan's storm three faith lessons as we have watched him soar in his faith.

First, a person of faith does not complain. They just call out to God. I have never heard Alan gripe to God about his condition. Sure, he has been broken but he has never complained. On the journey he has realized there are two options. One, to give up which complainers and gripers do most often; or two, you can call on Jesus.

As you face your storm, how do you react? Do you complain to God, or do you call out to Him? "Oh, I've called out and it didn't work for me." Did you really? How long did you cry out? One minute? One day? One week? One month? Here is a life lesson: You cry out until you get an answer. Here is another question: How did you cry out? Did you snap your fingers expecting God to jump or did you cry out in holy submission? I have watched Alan call out in holy submission, "Lord, teach me through this experience." He is on a journey and to him it is a journey of faith.

Another lesson he has taught our group is the importance of just following Jesus. The Psalmist gives an example of some mariners in a fierce storm in Psalm 107:23-30. In verses 28-30 we find the secret and the promise of God. Those who call on Him will be brought to where they desire. The Psalmist writes…

> Then they cried to the Lord in their trouble,
> and He brought them out of their distresses. He caused
> the storm to be still, so that the waves of the sea were
> hushed. Then they were glad because they were quiet;
> so He guided them to their desired haven.

What is every person's desired haven who find themselves in a fierce storm? It is a place of peace, serenity, hope, comfort, and rest; a place of joy and fulfillment. The storm may not be of your choosing but following Jesus will give you the haven you desire to be in.

The last lesson of faith Alan has taught us is that God's faithfulness is our fuel. When people fall by the wayside in the midst of their storm, it is usually when they didn't see hope in the future. When a person does not see hope in the future, he

WHEN A PERSON DOES NOT SEE HOPE IN THE FUTURE, HE USUALLY GIVES UP IN THE PRESENT. usually gives up in the present. Alan's faith is real, dynamic, and growing. His future is bright because God is real and Jesus is near. And while it may be a trite saying, Alan knows who holds the future.

Alan Fahring sums up his journey of faith in four ways. These are lessons he has learned:

Lesson #1: False gods give no answers during the storms of life. To trust in anything or anyone other than the true God of this universe will only ensure emptiness in a person's life and a deeper darkness in the midst of the struggle.

Lesson #2: One must discover God is real by entering a personal relationship with Him through His Son, Jesus Christ. On his journey Jesus has become very real to Alan. From the day of surgery forward Alan continues to discover something new about his Lord and also about his life. One of the greatest insights that I believe Alan has learned through adversity is that it is not the end. Adversity does not have to end in defeat. It can be the point of the greatest advancement in your own walk with God if you will let Him do His work in you. It must begin with a personal relationship with Jesus.

Lesson #3: Don't overlook the blessings. You are blessed! In every person's life storms have a tendency to make us, no force us, to look at our priorities. Everyone who has ever walked through a drastic storm understands how quickly one's priorities can change. Football for Alan had to take a lesser role. Faith, family, and friends have become the most stabilizing factors in his life.

When False Gods Give No Answers

Lesson #4: He came to understand everyone dies; therefore, live for maximum impact for Christ. Alan has sought to do so in ways that his health will allow. He has sought to serve the Lord. He has taken that same conquering spirit, focused it on his faith, and man, how God has used him as he has shared with others about his journey!

Alan's journey is not finished. On two occasions, he was given eighteen months to live; however, he has surpassed that by years. Currently, he is in an experimental program for his cancer at the National Health Institute in Washington, DC. God is using him in speaking up for Jesus with others. Alan understands it is Christ who is carrying him through.

FOOTPRINTS

One night a man had a dream. He dreamed he was walking along the beach with the Lord. Across the sky flashed scenes from his life. For each scene he noticed two sets of footprints in the sand. One belonging to him and the other to the LORD.

When the last scene of his life flashed before him, he looked back at the footprints in the sand. He noticed many times along the path of his life there were only one set of footprints. He also noticed that it happened at the very lowest and saddest times in his life.

This really bothered him and he questioned the LORD about it.

"LORD, you said that once I decided to follow You, You'd walk with me all the way. But I have noticed that during the most troublesome times in my life there is only one set of footprints. I don't understand why when I needed You the most, You would leave

me."

The LORD replied, "My precious, precious child, I love you and I would never leave. During your times of trial and suffering when you see only one set of footprints, it was then that I carried you." [1]

His old god could give no answer. His journey has taught him Jesus is always there to guide and fulfill every need. In the moments Alan feels like stumbling, the Lord picks him up and carries him with His righteous right hand.

Every person will be called upon to face storms, struggles, and adversity. How one chooses to handle these tells a lot about the person. Up to this point in his journey, Alan Fahring has proven what he has been all of his life—a winner. Traits he developed as a child have helped him greatly in his battle with cancer.

As a boy on the playgrounds of Salina, Kansas, he developed this value for his life, "If I'm going to participate, then I am to give it my all. I will do it as hard as I can as long as I can." Every day he gets up and moves to the line of scrimmage. For him the opponent is fierce and plays for keeps. Attitude spells it out loud for Alan. Remember, he has a heart of a lion. The heart of the lion roars across the line— "This is my game, my field. They will have to carry me off the field. I am never going to quit, I'm here to win!" Attitude is important in your fight with adversity.

For Alan Fahring, he can teach us all about positive attitudes when your back is to the wall. Remember, that is who he is—a coach. However, he has demonstrated even with a heart to win, the most important element in the battle is one's relationship with Christ. Those who were fighting the storm

When False Gods Give No Answers

on the troubled sea in Psalm 107 remind us if our trust is in the Lord, He will lead us to our desired haven. Alan knows this to be true, for in the midst of his storm God has given him peace, strength, hope, comfort, and rest. Alan has discovered these great benefits just by walking with his best friend - Jesus.

Are you facing storms or adversities in your life? Instead of crying out in defeat, you would do well to stop long enough to view it from God's perspective. In every storm God will use moments in the struggle to teach us godly traits and character. With every lesson we learn He is preparing us for a greater ministry to others who need to see Jesus. We must always remember God has a wonderful purpose for our lives. His goal is to conform our life to the likeness of Jesus. God allows

> **IN EVERY STORM GOD WILL USE MOMENTS IN THE STRUGGLE TO TEACH US GODLY TRAITS AND CHARACTER.**

storms to come our way to mold and shape us. He has done that wonderfully in the life of Alan Fahring. Today you see more of Jesus in his life. His god of 37 years had no answers but his friend, Jesus that he met at an FCA camp as a teenaged boy, has proven Himself more than able to meet the challenges of the storm. When the false gods of this world are incapable of giving any answers, there is Jesus. He is able.

Legacy

DYING TO LIVE

*What is lacking most in the lives of Christians today
is not a better living, but a better dying!
We need to die a thorough death.*
Watchman Nee

Christianity today is a far cry from those believers
who lived in the first century. When they came to Christ it
was a costly proposition. It was not the health, wealth and
prosperity gospel we hear so much of today in America. In
reality for most of those early believers it was a call to come
and die. Many of them were martyrs for the faith.

Church history has been sprinkled by the blood of these
early believers. The pages of history reveal some were boiled
to their death in vats of oil. Others were skinned alive and left
to die. There were others who were covered with tar and set
afire with torches around the Caesar's palace. Recorded for
us are the times when other believers were dragged to their
deaths by teams of wild horses. Others were eaten by wild
animals while others were sawn in two. All of these events were
caused by one thing. The followers of *the Way*, as they were
known, were subjected to these cruel forms of punishment
and death because of one commitment they had made. The
commitment was – to live for Jesus. There was no such thing
as casual Christianity in their day. In fact, part of their legacy
was astonishing. They were *dying to live* for Jesus!

With that as a backdrop, it is sad to see people who say
they love God with all their hearts and yet their lives do not

count much for the Kingdom. They sell out and compromise and the result is they waste a valuable life. How it must break the heart of God. He cries out, "But you don't understand! I really desire to use you in a tremendous way!" It's called making sure you're building a legacy.

When the Apostle Paul writes the church at Galatia, he addresses what has become known as his life verse. It has become known as his legacy. Paul states,

> *I have been crucified with Christ and it is no longer I who live, but Christ lives in me; and the life which I now live in the flesh I live by faith in the Son of God, who loved me, and delivered Himself up for me. (Galatians 2:20)*

I want you to see the emphasis. He says, "I've been crucified." Then he continues, "The life which I now live is no longer me but it's Jesus Christ living through my life."

Remember the lady who died and at her funeral, and the only thing I could say was that she loved race cars? What a waste of a life. Paul had no such problem. In his life we see a powerful legacy. The holy God of the universe made sure it was recorded for our benefit. As you study his life you discover the uniqueness of the man and what it was about him that left a tremendous mark on this world. Each of us will leave a mark on this world. It will be a godly mark or a worldly mark but a mark we will leave. God said that Noah found favor in the eyes of God. That's a legacy.

EACH ONE OF US WILL LEAVE A MARK ON THIS WORLD. IT WILL BE A GODLY MARK OR A WORDLY MARK BUT A MARK WE WILL LEAVE.

Dying to Live

Abraham was a friend of God. Enoch walked with God and David was a man after the heart of God. Well, what about Paul? What was said of him should be said of each of us.

Recall the scene once again when Maximus was about to lead his army into battle and challenged his men. He said, "Men, I want you to always remember that what we do in this life will echo throughout eternity." Allow that thought to resonate in the depths of your mind. What we do in this life will echo throughout eternity! I desire four things to echo throughout eternity when it comes to my life.

Think with me just for a moment. One day I am probably going to die. They are going to roll my body down to the front of North Metro and when they do my wife, Mary, and my son, Stephen, and daughter-in-law, Brooke, along with my son, Jonathan, and his wife, and Kristen and her husband as well as all my grandchildren and my great-grandchildren and my great-great-grandchildren are going to fill the mourner's bench. (I am ready to go; I just don't want to go on the next boat load!) All my preacher buddies will gather and stand to speak the truth concerning the hyphen that represents my life. I want them to be able to say four things about my life that I have learned from Paul's life.

SAVED

The first thing I want them to be able to say about my life concerns my salvation. I want them to be able to look at Mary and say "Mary, one thing we know about Frank, he was saved!" This is so important especially in the day in which we live. Billy Graham says as many as eighty percent of the people who sit in the average church on Sunday morning have never been born again. I believe it. When I look at people's lives, listen to the way they talk, and get a view of their behavior I agree with Billy Graham. There are many who fill churches each Sunday and claim to be a Christian and go right back into the world and live as though there is no Christ. They may look back on some weak experience somewhere in their life where they stake their claim but if there is no radical difference in their life there has been no Jesus.

A few years ago I was preaching in Athens, Georgia. A man stood to sing before I preached. Before the music started he looked at me and said, "Dr. Cox, we've never met but I've been saved because of your ministry." I looked at the man whom I had never laid eyes on before and listened as he explained. He said, "There is a man who recently was saved at your church by the name of Dan Blackwell. Well when Dan received Christ he came back to our place of work at Nash Chevrolet and started a Bible study. In the Bible study, I finally came to understand that I had never given my heart and life to Jesus Christ. When I was a little boy I used to go to Mount Tabor Baptist Church in Duluth, Georgia. At the age of twelve, we were in a revival and my mother saw all my buddies going down and giving their lives to Jesus. She leaned down to me and whispered, 'Now honey, don't you think it's time for you to go and give your heart to Jesus?'" He said he sat there and looked up at his mother as she continued, "Now son, I've been watching you and I know that you want that hunting knife down at the hardware store. So if you'll go on down tonight and give your heart to Jesus Christ, I'll buy you that hunting knife tomorrow." He said, "Preacher, if I would have died between that night and the other day when I gave my heart and life to Jesus over at Nash Chevrolet, I would have busted hell wide open because I would have been saved by a hunting knife!"

Do you know there are many including those who may be reading this book who, when they get real honest with themselves, have been saved by something equally as heretical. Maybe you just walked down an aisle in an emotionally charged service and went through the process but never dealt with your lostness and the meaning of the atoning work of Jesus. You never repented of your sin; therefore, all you did was walk down an aisle and got wet in a baptismal pool. You never have turned away from your life of sin and given your heart to Jesus. What is the tragedy? I will tell you what the tragedy is – false assurance. If you were to die today you are not ready to meet Jesus.

Let me share an experience with you. I think about the man I met in Wrens, Georgia in a church where I was preaching a revival. Each night of the revival I made this statement: "In every person's life there must be a time, point and place where you can point back to and make the following statement. This is where I recognized I was a sinner in need of a Savior. I repented of my sin and invited Christ into my life as my Lord and Savior." On the last night of the revival the church was packed to capacity. I preached on the wrath of God. I drove home the need for every person to receive Christ. At the invitation 26 people responded to Jesus.

As I walked out of that building to return home, there was an older gentleman just kind of standing off waiting for me. He almost looked troubled as he spoke, "Brother Frank, would you come here for a minute?" I agreed and walked over and stuck out my hand. I was expecting him to say, "Man, what a great night we had", but instead he said, "I don't like your preaching." I was kind of rocked by that statement as

I looked into his weary eyes. I asked him what he meant. I was expecting him to say what they usually say, I'm loud and fast, and I knew what to say if he said that, instead he looked at me and said, "I have a problem with your preaching for this reason. Every single night this week you've said if there hasn't been a time, point and place you could go back to and say that's where I recognized that I was a sinner, that's where I realized that Jesus Christ was the only Messiah and that's where I turned from my sins and accepted Him as Lord and Savior and if there is not a time, point and place then you're lost." I listened as he continued and told me he had never had such an experience but knew he would go to heaven if he died. According to him there was never a day in his life he did not believe in Jesus. Well, I thought to myself even the demons of hell believe Jesus is the Son of God. His next statement sent chills up and down my spine. "I grew up in a Christian home. I have evolved into being a Christian and I know I am heaven bound!" After taking a deep breath I assured him he would not go to heaven but to hell. He then proceeded to tell me of all the wonderful things he had done in his life. Sunday school teacher, deacon, disaster relief; on and on the list went. He would be considered one of the best his community had to offer and especially his church. But he was still lost.

> **WHEN A PERSON RECEIVES CHRIST AS LORD AND SAVIOR THERE WILL BE A MAJOR POINT OF CONVICTION IN THEIR LIFE CONCERNING THEIR LOSTNESS.**

There is no evolution to salvation. Believe me when a person receives Christ as Lord and Savior there will be a major point of conviction in their life concerning their lostness. There will be a confrontation by the

Dying to Live

Holy Spirit as He draws them toward the Savior. When Paul comes to Galatians 2 and says "I have been crucified" he was saying "I've been saved." You know what he was thinking about? He was thinking about that moment on that Damascus Road experience when the blinding light came down and he encountered Jesus Christ first hand. Jesus said, "Saul, Saul, why are you persecuting Me?" (Acts 9:4). At that moment in time was the time, point and place where conviction fell upon Saul and he was radically saved.

Recently our church moved into our new Worship Center. I was called by a newspaper reporter concerning this accomplishment in our congregation's life. She caught me off guard when she made this statement. She said "Your church members say you're not like other mega-church pastors." I inquired what she meant. She said, "They tell me you haven't watered down the Gospel. They say you can still come to your church and feel conviction." She reminded me in this day and time preachers have forsaken the preaching of the Gospel and the altar call for people to be convicted and converted. Without the conviction of their sin there will be no repentance and conversion. I firmly believe there's going to be many people in the very bowels of hell that one day will cry out to this generation of preachers and say "Why didn't you warn us that we could come to a place like this?" My job is not to entertain; my job is to preach the Word of God under the anointing of God in order to call men to a saving faith in Jesus. Adrian Rogers was right when he said, "We need God-called men who will take the Book of God and preach the Son of God with the anointing of the Spirit of God! We need men with warm hearts, wet eyes, clear heads and tongues set on fire." [1]

175

I looked at that man in Wrens, Georgia and said "Sir, you're going to bust hell wide open." We must understand there is no evolution in regards to one's salvation. It is a decision based upon a conviction that you are a sinner and that you need Jesus Christ as your Lord and Savior. Are you saved today? Or are you just a person who casually attends church with no spiritual relationship with Christ at all? Are you saved today or do you look back and say "Well, my mama took me to the nursery"? Are you saved today or is it that you have some testimony that says "Well, one day my mother promised me a hunting knife if I would just go down and be baptized"? Not good enough! You must come by way of Jesus, repenting of your sins and accept Him as Lord and Savior. Paul could write with confidence: "I have been crucified with Christ!"

SURRENDERED

Paul doesn't stop there. In verse 20 he shares a quality I pray they will be able to say about me. Paul states the fact that he was surrendered to the Lordship of Christ.

As the minister shares, I want him to look into the eyes of Stephen and Brooke and say, "Another thing we know about your dad is that he was totally surrendered." Let me ask you a question: Have you surrendered everything to Jesus Christ? Look at verse 20. Here is what Paul said, "I have been crucified with Christ, it is no longer I who live but it's Jesus living through me." You want spiritual warfare? When you start talking about abandonment, when you start talking about dying to self, when you start talking about surrendering everything to the Lordship of Jesus Christ, watch and see if the demons of hell don't show up at some point in your life.

Dying to Live

Do you know why? They don't want you to turn your life totally over to the Lordship of Jesus Christ. They want you to still live for the almighty dollar. They want you to still live for the possessions of this world. They want you to still live for your own agendas instead of living for the agendas and will of God. Paul had the concept of the Christian life down. He was totally surrendered to the Lordship of Christ. Paul says "It's no longer I who live, it's Jesus living through me". He was totally abandoned to Jesus Christ.

Let me tell you what I have learned as a Christian by personal experience. If you will learn this you will discover a great secret to the Christian life. Obedience to Christ and His Lordship is the key that secures the door of one's heart that keeps victory in and evil out. I have also learned that disobedience in one's life is the key that unlocks the door of one's heart and lets victory out and evil in. Write that down in the front of your Bible or on a note pad somewhere, but whatever you do write it down and commit it to memory!

> **OBEDIENCE TO CHRIST AND HIS LORDSHIP IS THE KEY THAT SECURES THE DOOR OF ONE'S HEART THAT KEEPS VICTORY IN AND EVIL OUT.**

Our world is littered with men who used to be preachers, great men of God. What tragic stories! Their stories are all so familiar. Somewhere life they became a little disobedient and a crack began to appear in the armor of their life. Maybe it was just a wrong thought. Immediately the demons of hell jumped all over it and began to lay the groundwork to destroy the lives and the ministries of these men. By their own admission, they coddled wrong and tempting thoughts and before long that crack in the armor grew wider and their victory was lost.

Satan is a rat and don't you ever forget it.

On the bayous of Louisiana they grow some of the biggest rats seen by man. When I was pastoring on the bayous of this sportsman's paradise, I was introduced to some of these creatures. They were huge unlike the Georgia mice I was accustomed to. One day my wife came running into my office and jumped up on my sofa and said, "You've got to do something about that rat!" Being a man's man that I am, I thought to myself, "Why don't you do something about that rat?" She said, "There's a big rat running down the hallway!" I grabbed a broom handle and started down to where she said she encountered this creature. I was standing outside the door and I knew I had to go in and be the man for my wife so I prayed a simple prayer, "Lord, I'm going in. One of us is not coming out. I beg your protection upon my life." I went in swinging and ran the rat down the hall. I had him cornered ready to lay the lethal blow when one of the Cajun women walked into the hallway. She said, "Brother Frank, what are you doing, man?" I said, "I'm about to kill this rat!" I turned and the rat was gone. She said, "You don't know anything about rats, do you?" I asked what she meant. She said, "Frank, anywhere a rat can stick its nose, it can pull its body, no matter how big the body is." That inspired me! When my wife and I made our way home from our church that night I stopped at K-Mart and bought masking tape, electrical tape, freezer tape, every other kind of tape I could lay my hands on. I went home and sealed up every crack in our apartment because I didn't want any rats in our apartment!

Some of you are allowing the wicked rat, Satan, into your life because of your disobedience. When he sees a little rebellion and senses a disobedient spirit and watches for the

Dying to Live

little crack in the armor of your life, he scurries to summons some demons to attack as he sets out to destroy you.

John, the gospel writer, warns us concerning the ploy of Satan. He writes, "The thief does not come except to steal, and to kill, and to destroy." Jesus then says, "I have come that they may have life, and that they may have it more abundantly" (John 10:10). So Satan will work overtime to lure you through a little disobedience onto the slippery slope toward destruction. That's the reason there are many who used to be a deacon, Sunday school teacher, or used to sing in the choir. Yes, some even used to preach. You ask them, "Why did you stop?" The answer is simple. Somewhere they allowed Satan to distract and destroy them. As a result they quit surrendering their all to Jesus. Are you surrendered totally to His Lordship? It may be that you need to sit back and close your eyes for a few moments and allow these words to flow through your mind to your heart to once again arrest your will and soul.

> **SATAN WILL WORK OVERTIME TO LURE YOU THROUGH A LITTLE DISOBEDIENCE ONTO THE SLIPPERY SLOPE TOWARD DESTRUCTION.**

All to Jesus I surrender,
All to Him I freely give;
I will ever love and trust Him,
In His presence daily live.
All to Jesus I surrender,
Lord I give myself to thee;
Fill me with thy love and power;
Let thy blessings fall on me.
I surrender all, I surrender all;

*All to thee my blessed Savior,
I surrender all.* [2]

Watchman Nee was correct – "We need to die a thorough death!"

SEEKER

There is a third thing I want to be said about my life. I want them to look at Jonathan and his precious wife and say, "Jonathan, there's a third thing we know about your Dad. He was a seeker after the mind of God." I want it to be said that I was serious about knowing God's mind through the study of Scripture.

Everyone who is serious about their walk with God should seek after the truth that is found in the Word of God. Have you read Psalm 1 lately?

> *How blessed is the man who does not walk in the counsel of the wicked, nor stand in the path of sinners, nor sit in the seat of scoffers! But his delight is in the law of the Lord, and in His law he meditates day and night. Whatever they do they prosper! (Psalm 1:1)*

Don't you want to be one who prospers? I know I sure do. It should be the desire of every Christian.

The Psalmist explains how to prosper. The secret is found in second verse. You must delight in the Word of God. Let me tell you about that word *delight*. When my first wife, Debbie, died of a malignant brain tumor in 1986, I really thought my life was finished. There was no more laughter in my life and for sure no joy. The heart of our home was gone. It was just a few months after Debbie's death God brought my present wife, Mary, into my and Stephen's life. She has been a special gift from God. She brought happiness and joy back into the lives of two hurting guys. When she is with me and I am sharing our story, I will point to her and say – "I delight in Mary!" Here is what that word means. She is precious to me – I hold her in high regard – I worship the ground she walks on because of what she has done for me and Stephen. In the same way a child of God delights in the law of the Lord. It means we hold the Word of God up as our authority. It is precious to us because it carries all the answers to this thing called life. It leads us to worship the God it reveals to us. It leads us to eternal life through the atonement of God's son, Jesus Christ. We delight in the law of God.

The Psalmist does not stop there. He says he also meditates upon the laws of God day and night. The word *meditate* is an interesting word out of the Hebrew. It is the same thing as a cow chewing its cud.

One night I was explaining this in a sermon in Athens, Georgia and a PhD in cowology from the University of Georgia came to hear me speak. I said, "You get a cow up early in the morning and feed her..." He said, "Frank, that sermon illustration is about 99% correct." I said, "Close enough." He said, "You don't get a cow up in the morning." I don't know what you do to a cow. I am a city boy. As far as I know you go in the barn, pull back the covers, shoo the cow up. You get her out there and feed her. I don't know what you feed the cow. Grass? Grains? Soybeans? Happy Meals from McDonald's? I don't know, but you feed a cow and they say when that cow gets out there in the heat of the day, it regurgitates what it has already eaten and chews on it and swallows it a second time and it goes down to a second stomach. Then after awhile you'll see the cow over in the shade and it will spit it up again and chew on it some more and swallow it and it goes down to a third stomach. After awhile that cow will vomit it up again and chew on it some more and swallow it – you know why? That PhD in cowology said it is getting all the strength from that food so it can stand and survive in the heat of the day.

Do you know why in the Holy Scriptures we are told to digest the Word of God? So when you are faced with temptation, when Satan is standing right before you and the demons of hell are trying to destroy you, what one should do is bring back up the Word of God that you have already digested into your life and meditate on it again so that you can stand against evil in the day of temptation. That is why you ought to be a seeker after the mind of God. We are to delight and meditate in the law of God. I want it to be said – "Frank sought the mind of God!"

SOUL WINNER

The last thing I want them to say about me is that I was a soul winner. I want them to be able to look at Kristen and her husband and say, "The fourth thing we know about your Dad was that he shared his faith in a dynamic way so people could come to know Jesus Christ as Lord and Savior." It is my desire to be faithful in sharing my faith – don't you?

I want to ask you a question. Who has recently come down the aisle of your church where you attend and said they have given their heart and life to Jesus because you led them to Him? Who is it? "Well, preacher, we're not the hired gun, that's your job!" Yet Jesus is plain in the Scripture. Jesus said,

Dying to Live

"Follow Me, and I will make you become fishers of men"(Mark 1:17). He said if you follow Him that He will make you to become a fisher of men. It will happen as you obey Him and live to His Lordship.

There is also a flip side of this phrase as well. Could it be that if you are not fishing for men, you are not following Him? We all know the truth of that question. The most dynamic thing you could ever do as a Christian is tell somebody else how to come to know Jesus as Lord and Savior. Do you know the greatest thing you could ever do for that lost person you work with is one day get up the nerve to bring up Jesus? The greatest thing you could ever do for that family member is tell them how to find real life through Jesus.

> **THE MOST DYNAMIC THING YOU COULD EVER DO AS A CHRISTIAN IS TELL SOMEBODY ELSE HOW TO COME TO KNOW JESUS AS LORD AND SAVIOR.**

I want to ask you a question. If those around you who do not have a personal relationship with Jesus have to wait for you to tell them about Christ, how long will they have to wait? How many of them will die and go to a real place called Hell because of our disobedience in this area of sharing Jesus.

The North American Mission Board Evangelism Department tells us that 95% of all Southern Baptists will go to their graves never telling anyone about Jesus. We go to church and sing songs encouraging the saint to go and tell the most wonderful story of the ages and yet we seldom respond in obedience. We have pastors who love to preach, deacons who want to deac, staff members who love to plan programs, Sunday school teachers who love to dispense Bible knowledge, but not many who are willing to go out and tell the unchurched how to come to Jesus. You say, "Frank, I don't see that in Galatians 2:20." Everywhere Paul went, he told about Jesus. People responded by giving their lives to Christ and many times they established a church. We should always be sharing our faith in Jesus Christ. Who is it that you're burdened for? Who is it that you'd like to see come to know Jesus Christ as Lord and Savior?

Many years ago in New Orleans, Louisiana they were building Interstate 10 right near the Super Dome. One day there came a cry and the work stopped because one of the men, who had been working on the construction crew had not been paying attention as a cement truck was backing up. When he caught a glimpse of the truck coming right at him he scurried to get out of the way but fell and the truck backed over him.

Men on the construction crew ran to him to help as they waited for the emergency help to arrive. The man who knelt down beside the dying man and held his head in his lap was a Christian but had never been one to share his faith. The dying man looked at him and with a fainting voice asked 'Tell me how I can go to Heaven?'" The Christian said, "I looked into his eyes and was stunned. I did not know how to tell him how to go to Heaven and I watched my friend as he breathed his last, destined for hell!"

Who is it in your life? Who is it in your life that needs Jesus as their Lord and Savior? Will you be a soul winner?

God watches everything about you. He records your legacy for all eternity. I pray that your legacy will be outstanding in the eyes of God.

When you go to the cemetery, to the grave of a loved one, there are several things that are important on that headstone.

Dying to Live

There is the birth date of that precious person and there is an ending date. The most important part is the hyphen that represents the life they lived. When you look at that hyphen it's either going to bring up great memories of a life well lived or either it's going to bring up a lot of distraught memories of a wasted life. It is my prayer that when my loved ones visit my grave and stare at my hyphen they will say – "Man, Frank's life made a difference."

What will be your legacy? Noah found favor in the eyes of God. Abraham was a friend of God. Enoch walked with God. David was a man after God's own heart. Paul says "I've been saved. I'm surrendered." He sought the mind of God. He shared his faith. What will they say about you?

Mama just loved race cars. She lived 52 years on this earth and the only thing I could say about her was that she loved a hunk of metal and an engine. What has God written about your life at this point? What will be your conclusion?

Until you are dying to live for Jesus you are not ready to build a dynamic legacy.

Legacy

ENDNOTES

Chapter 1 – A Call to An Extraordinary Life

1. Jonathan Edwards, *The Resolutions of Jonathan Edwards*, Internet, Center for Reformed Theology and Apologetics, 1996-2006.

2. James Emery White, *Life-Defining Moments*, (Waterbrook Press, Colorado Springs, 2001), p. 3.

3. Robert Herrick, *Works of Robert Herrick, Vol. 1*, Alfred Pollard, ed. (Lawrence & Bullen, Laudrea, 1891), p. 102.

4. Touchstone Pictures copyrighted feature film, *Dead Poets Society*, Disney Enterprises, Inc.

5. Ibid.

Chapter 2 – Mama Loved Race Cars

1. Dewey Gram, *Gladiator*, screenplay by David Franzoni, John Logan, and William Nicholson, Gladiator (Onyx, New York, 2000), p. 24.

2. Ibid

3. Po Bronson, *What Should I Do With My Life?* (Random House, New York, 2002), XV.

4. Michael Best, *Shakespeare's Life and Times*, Internet Shakespeare Editions, Unitversity of Victoria: Victoria, BC, 2001-2005.

5. Gram, *Gladiator*, p. 24.

6. Ibid

7. Ibid

Chapter 3 – Noah: The Favored One!
1.   Matthew 24:36-51
2.   Bruce Wilkerson, *Set Apart: Discovering Personal Victory Through Holiness* (Sisters, Oregon, Multnomah Publishers, 1998, 2003), p. 69.

Chapter 4 – Abraham: The Friend of God
1.   Bill Bright, *The Joy of Active Prayer* (Victor, Colorado Springs, 2005), p. 31.
2.   John Guest, "Only A Prayer Away", *Christianity Today*, Vol. 40.
3.   Brit Hume, Interview with the President, MSNBC, 2004.
4.   Charles Wesley, *Short Hymns on Select Passages of Holy Scripture*, 1762.

Chapter 5 – David: A Man after God's Heart
1.   Frank Cox, *Trusting God's Heart* (Baxter Press, Friendwood, Texas, 2000), p. 10.

Chapter 6 – Enoch: Walked with God
1.   Robert Baker, "Country Road 13", *Christianity Today*, Vol. 40.
2.   Sybil Stanton, "Purpose", *Leadership Magazine*
3.   Oswald Chambers, *My Utmost for His Highest* Updated Edition, (Discovery House Publishers, Grand Rapids, Michigan, 1992), November 18.
4.   Ibid

Chapter 7 – Shadrach, Meshach and Abednego:
The Semper Fidelis Gang

1. Edythe Draper, *Draper's Book of Quotations for the Christian World* (Tyndale House Publishers, Inc.,Wheaton, Illinois, 1992) Entry 8801.
2. Ibid, Entry 8802
3. Bob Barnes, *Men Under Construction* (Harvest House Publishers, Eugene, Oregon, 2006), p. 201.
4. Draper, *Book of Quotations for the Christian World*, entry 8805.
5. Barnes, *Men Under Construction*, p. 45.
6. Ibid, p. 169.

Chapter 8 – Blessed Brokenness

1. Henry Blackaby, *Experiencing God* (Broadman & Holman, Nashville, Tennessee, 1994), p. 214
2. Frank Cox, *Trusting God's Heart* (Baxter Press, Friendswood, Texas, 2000), p. 129.

Chapter 9 – When False Gods Give No Answers

1. "Footprints in the Sand" is a poem that has been in the public domain for years. There are three variations of the poem in existence. There are three different poets who in recent years have claimed to be the author of the poem. They are Mary Stevenson, *Footprints in the Sand*, 1936. Carolyn Carty, *Footprints*, 1963. Margaret Fishback Powers, 1964. For this book the author chose Carolyn Carty's – *Footprints*, 1963.

Chapter 10 – Dying to Live

1. Adrian Rogers, *Messages on Preaching*, (Bellevue Baptist Church, Memphis, Tennessee).

2. Judson W. Van DeVenter, *I Surrender All*, 1896 (Convention Press, Nashville, Tennessee, 1975), p. 347.

ABOUT THE AUTHOR

Frank Cox became Senior Pastor of North Metro First Baptist Church in 1980. Since his arrival the church has become known as one of the fastest growing Southern Baptist churches in Georgia. Through these 26 years of ministry God has given the church a diverse ministry in reaching many different segments of the community. Dr. Cox is very involved in the community serving as chaplain of the Collins Hill High School football team, and serves on the Advisory Council for the Collins Hill cluster. He speaks to youth encampments, evangelism conferences, revivals, and crusades as well as student bodies at colleges, universities, and seminaries throughout America. His preaching ministry has also taken him to Russia, Guatemala, and Moldova.

Dr. Cox attended Truett-McConnell College in Cleveland, Georgia, received a B.A. degree in religion from Mercer University, a Master of Divinity degree from New Orleans Baptist Theological Seminary, and a Doctor of Ministry degree from Luther Rice Seminary.

He has served as President of the Georgia Baptist Convention, and has served that convention in several other positions. He has served on the Executive Committees of both the Georgia Baptist Convention and the Southern Baptist Convention. In addition, Dr. Cox has served on the boards for several ministries including the David Ring Evangelistic Ministry and currently serves as Chairman of the Georgia Baptist Health Care Ministry Foundation. He has spoken for chapel services for corporations such as Gold Kist, Inc., and Injoy. He was elected and served as First Vice President of the Southern Baptist Convention.

Dr. Cox and his wife, Mary, are the proud parents of three children: Stephen, who is married to Brooke, Jonathan and Kristen. The family lives in Lawrenceville, Georgia.